PRAISE FOR RUBY McCONNELL'S *WILDERNESS AND THE AMERICAN SPIRIT*

"Ruby McConnell sings a landscape from a place of stillness and reflection, improvising from talismans she finds along the Applegate Trail. *Wilderness and the American Spirit* is an engaging meditation about the need for a new consciousness between humans and the earth."

—**PETER STARK**, author of *Gallop Toward the Sun, The Last Empty Places* and *Astoria*

"Through capacious and warm-hearted storytelling, Ruby McConnell lights up the ley lines that criss-cross the West from the notorious Humboldt Sink in Northeastern Nevada to McConnell's own Willamette Valley in Western Oregon. She introduces and re-introduces early settlers and back-to-the-landers and festival-goers and a particularly sweet and tragic Mouseketeer. But these stories are not single-note—they are not only heroic or ill-fated or profiteering or idealistic or tragic. Rather, they are the stories of how each of these flawed adventurers brushes up against landscape and culture and moments in time and how, together, they form a narrative web—one strand shimmering to the next—that tells the story of a nation."

—**WENDY WILLIS**, author of *These are Strange Times My Dear: Field Notes from the Republic*

"Ruby McConnell's book is a lyrical sampler of the history of the west and its wild spirit. McConnell beautifully muses on the call of the wild, why Americans have answered it over and over again, and the dangers of the myth of wilderness. Beginning with settlers and cowboys and moving through the environmental movement, hippies, and Burning Man, this book explores what the west means and what people have found upon their arrival from pre-contact eras to modern times."

—**TOVE DANOVICH**, journalist and author of *Under the Henfluence*

"In a sweeping yet succinct volume, Ruby McConnell tells the much-needed story of how the United States came to be so vast and yet so meticulously measured, giving context and richness to American history chestnuts like the Oregon Trail and Manifest Destiny. She wraps these facts with a riveting Westward ho-narrative about the Applegate Trail that makes the universal very personal for those who trekked it, and reading about it a nail-biting experience. She weaves in the Trump years, an unsolved murder, Burning Man, and the pandemic as signposts along the way to her conclusion.

With her scientist's eye, McConnell encompasses the history of land surveys in America and around the world, the land itself in all its rich formations, and what has happened to this land as pioneers and their descendants have trodden and reproduced down to this day and time, when the climate change clock is already past the alarm stage. McConnell brings myth and legend together with brutal reality, and it works like a charm. Beautiful, rich work from one of America's bright new literary lights."

—**JULIA PARK TRACEY**, author of *The Bereaved*

"Ruby McConnell offers a rich and nuanced telling of US ideas about land, the Frontier, identity, and so many of the individual and social experiences that have led us to the difficult moment we live within.

It has become clear that our collective relationships to one another, to place, to the environment, to justice, to the threads that make up contemporary society desperately need to be re-spun, re-thought, and re-told. Read this book through to the end to develop new maps and topographies for other ways of being part of the story of the United States. We urgently need this kind of great storytelling."

—**DAVID SYRING**, Fellow, Institute on the Environment

WILDERNESS
& THE AMERICAN SPIRIT

WILDERNESS & THE AMERICAN SPIRIT

RUBY McCONNELL

Overcup Press

Wilderness & the American Spirit

Published in 2024

Cover Art: Cole Gerst
Book Design: Jenny Kimura

'Applegate Trail Map' modified from 'Oregon Trail' map from Atlas of Oregon, Second Edition, © 2001 University of Oregon and used with permission.

ISBN: 979-8-9856527-6-5

Library of Congress Control Number: 2023949577

Printed in China

Overcup Press
4207 SE Woodstock Blvd. #253
Portland, OR 97206

Overcupbooks.com
Rubymcconnell.com

CONTENTS

*For Paul, who walks
this road with me.*

LAND AND FIRST PEOPLES ACKNOWLEDGMENT

THE AMERICAN WEST WAS FORCIBLY TAKEN FROM ITS Indigenous inhabitants. This book is not a comprehensive history of the United States and does not attempt tell the complete story of Indigenous peoples of the United States. That is not intended to diminish their experiences or the importance of their history, culture, and people to the United States today and from its inception. But it is to say that as a white woman, as a first-generation American who lives on unceded Kalapuya land, it is not my story to tell. It is, however, important and critical history to learn, and it's important that it be learned from Indigenous voices, of which there are many. The author encourages readers of this book to invest in Indigenous peoples by purchasing their work, reading their stories, and taking appropriate action, particularly in the restoration of land promised by treaty.

ESSENTIAL READING ON INDIGENOUS PEOPLES OF THE UNITED STATES BY INDIGENOUS AUTHORS

The Winona LaDuke Reader by Winona LaDuke

The Heartbeat of Wounded Knee: Native America from 1890 to the Present by David Treur

As Long as Grass Grows: The Indigenous Fight for Environmental Justice, from Colonization to Standing Rock by Dina Gilio-Whitaker

Custer Died for Your Sins: An Indian Manifesto by Vine Deloria Jr.

An Indigenous Peoples' History of the United States by Roxanne Dunbar-Ortiz

Our History is the Future by Nick Estes

INTRODUCTION

THE AMERICAN SPIRIT IN ENVIRONMENTALISM

THE FIRST MAPS WERE OF THE STARS. IMAGES OF THE NIGHT sky and its constellations that date back tens of thousands of years have been found painted and etched into the sides of caves in sites across Europe. They are reminders that humans have always looked into the vast infinity of the universe and wondered about their role and place in it. In this way, map-making is a form of storytelling. Just as the rock record serves as the biography of the landscape, maps record the history of our knowledge and understanding of the world around us at distinct points in time. Early maps placed humanity in the center of the world, cementing in our psyches the idea of ourselves as disproportionately important.

In time, maps became largely symbolic in nature, the narrative tools of the wealthy and powerful. By the Medieval period, maps, especially those of Europe, were little more than cosmological diagrams, depicting the world as a single continent drifting in an ocean surrounded by images of Heaven and Hell. It wasn't until the last few hundred years that maps as we conceive of them today became commonly used as navigational tools. The earliest of those maps were charted to aid exploration and seizure of foreign lands by western empires. They were intended to guide their users to safety.

Maps though, even scientifically based maps, are fallible and can say more about the people who make or rely on them than of the places they depict. Often, as in the case of those carried and later created by Christopher Columbus, they are fiction; sometimes they depict nothing at all. For centuries inland North America was a land unmapped by the very people attempting to possess it. It was a terra incognita, a vast blankness across a page—the infinite unknown.

It was into this infinite unknown the first Americans cast their fate, tying to it all of their notions of the order of the universe and the human and patriotic spirit. It would become a defining characteristic of a yet-to-be-born country, the American infinity: infinite time, space, land, and resources. For a long time, it was possible to seize these infinities with both hands, our greed and hungry disregard for consequences or the fate of future generations remaining tempered by lack of population. Today, from the forward edge of environmental crisis, it is easy to see that it was an illusion.

From the vantage of the twenty-first century, it is possible see how our infinities, and our navigation of them, have driven us to species-wide suicidal behaviors that have resulted in climate change, resource depletion, systemic environmental injustice, critical failures of water and air quality, food instability, and health and addiction crises. Now, as the broader results of pushing into infinity, of always wanting to fill the map, unfold, the American role in the environmental crisis has been revealed—and it is uniquely tied to issues of patriotic and religious spirit. In that way, the environmental crisis is also a spiritual crisis and must be talked about and approached from that context. The consequences of our collective actions over time are directly impacting each of us, sickening our bodies and dampening even our most basic forms of spirit: hope and resilience. It's a self-perpetuating cycle. This sickening of the spirit, this loss of hope, is what allows us to take no action, turn away from the rising tide, the endangered owl, the smoke from distant wildfires. It is why we can persist in polluting our natural lifelines and even our own bodies.

No more. The transition from the age of warning to the age of consequence through which we are all living necessitates an environmental paradigm, ethic, and course of action different from anything we have had in the past. It necessitates a new, postmillennial environmentalism, a secular liturgy of the land.

How do we get there?

First must come the breakdown of harmful tropes, cultural appropriation, and colonial constructs that problematically informed and characterized most nineteenth- and twentieth-century environmental movements and philosophies, especially with respect to discussions of belief systems, politics, and matters of the human spirit. In the twenty-first century, it is widely acknowledged that environmental issues *are* social justice issues.

Then, we need a new environmental canon. One filled with new ways of talking about issues of the environment, new voices, new stories, and new solutions. Here, in this volume, you get me, a second-generation environmental geologist and activist, a feminist writer and artist who was raised as a Catholic in the liberal valleys of the Pacific Northwest and steeped in the folklore and traditions of the Irish Celts.

Pre-Christian Irish Celts believed in the universal sacredness of all things and that the divine pervaded every aspect of the world, imbuing everything, people, plants, and even stones with spirit. They had a love of the mystical and the poetic and they were progressive, elevating women as druidesses and priestesses. They believed in the power of storytelling; the Irish Seanchaí (wayfaring storytellers) were keepers of myth and legend, educators, historians, and fortune tellers. The Seanchaí held all the knowledge of history and culture and interpreted its lessons, illuminating the path of the people. The stories and discussion presented in the following pages are intended to do the same: to present a framework for a discussion of the ways in which human, particularly American, wellness and environment are intertwined—how they share the breath, or spirit, of the world.

Geography and maps play important parts in this framework, and not just in the connection between the Seanchaí and me, your geologist-storyteller in this journey. In many ways the story of the United States begins with the Celts, who were dispersed across central Europe, the same part of the world that transported the first colonists to North America. Celtic spirituality holds a particular place for those who left home and family behind and went out into the world as first colonists, then westering emigrants. Most especially, Celtic lore acknowledges the journeys of those who make pilgrimages to ancient or sacred sites, "thin places" where there seemed to be only a veil between this world and the spirit world. In the American landscape, the West, especially the far west, has always been such a place, associated with fears and myths and legends and the unknown, the infinity into which the American Dream has always been cast.

In the twenty-first century, the West, in the modern mind, has become the Old West, a caricature of bygone times at best, a harbor of colonialism and oppression at worst. But for all the truth in that assessment, the West is still the lifeblood of the economy, an essential land from which we continue to draw our dwindling abundances, and the stage on which our partisan politics and divided values plays out. Perhaps because of that, thin places still exist in the American West. The Applegate Trail is one of those places.

Largely forgotten from history, the Applegate Trail extends from southern Oregon to Humboldt, Nevada, and connects the Oregon and California Trails. It was the longest, most heavily traveled route of western migration in American history, and today has dropped from public consciousness, making it a modern terra incognita. The land it traverses still bears the scars of humanity's crossing and many of the country's biggest environmental battles and social ills have come to a head along its route. And because so much of environmental thought, activism, and culture, has come out of the American West—Gary Snyder, Barry Lopez, Wendell Berry, Aldo Leopold, Edward Abbey—the Applegate Trail, cutting as it does through the very heart of that country, serves as a potent microcosm for the story of the American landscape since the arrival of Europeans. The story of the Applegate Trail and the stories of the people, places, and even the land itself from along its route can tell us a lot about who we are, how we got here, and what path forward we should take.

Previous environmental philosophies, movements, and polices have failed to pull us from the forward edge of consequence. It's time for a new, environmental cosmology that addresses the fallacy of the infinite and a new, postmillennial environmentalism rooted in the direct action of individuals and motivated by the informed understanding of environmental systems and conditions and shared human story. Environmentalism as a movement must shift from exposition into a tradition of storytelling and memory activism with the purpose of encouraging people to find the ways in which their lives are connected to nature, reestablish the integrity of that connection, and heal themselves and ultimately the environment.

What you will find here is history and science intertwined with stories of people and places, flights of fancy intermingled with calls to action. Here I tell you stories of the ways that people, mostly men, and of those, almost entirely white men, arrived, claimed, and proceeded to use and behave in the American West. It is a journey intended to be an illumination of how the "American spirit," in its broadest possible definition, has shaped the land and our relationship to it. This is an honest look at the people who populated and seized power in the terra incognita and how they, we, rendered it such a broken, depleted, and divided land. It is an essential filling-in of the map of the American relationship to the landscape, and it is how we will chart a new course.

Join me.

ONE

A HUMBLE FENCE, 1492–1800

"Hispaniola is a miracle. Mountains and hills, plains and pastures, are both fertile and beautiful...there are many wide rivers of which the majority contain gold."

—CHRISTOPHER COLUMBUS

EMIGRATION WEST IN THE UNITED STATES, AS A PRACTICE, has always been a colonial endeavor. The earliest European arrivals to North America had voyaged west to discover "new worlds" and new passages, routes that would lead them, they hoped, to points in the Far East. The goal was to establish new silk roads via westward routes. Trade, though, requires capital, as does expedition and discovery in often dangerous lands. Any passages west, they knew, would have to first be paved in gold. So, when Columbus set sail from Spain in 1492, he did so with only that one true goal foremost in his mind: gold. Queen Isabella and King Ferdinand had just defeated the Moors, finally reclaiming Spain as a Catholic monarchy after seven hundred years of war. Now they were casting out Jews and Muslims who they saw as conquerors and oppressors. It was an expensive endeavor. They thought there might be fortune in the lands rumored to exist across the ocean to the west. Columbus saw an opportunity and was eager to please. Thirsty for gold himself, he exaggerated, promising "as much gold as they need" if only the monarchs could find it in their hearts and purses to finance the voyage. In a place so vast, how could there not be gold? They agreed, and for hundreds of years, so did everyone else who set sail to peck at the edges of this vast new place.

It was in this way that the modern American relationship to the land began, before any Europeans had even set foot on it, in the imaginations of sailors, explorers, and monarchs, driven west by power and greed toward a gilded dream. But wildness, not gold, was what they found, or at least how they described it. Filled with unknowns and danger, the whole New World was, as early explorers described, a tangled mass of impassable terrain, unidentifiable plants and animals, unpassable rivers, and land—more and more land however far west they pushed. There was an abundance of nearly everything, except, it seemed, gold. For that, they pressed on. Deeper west, deeper into the wildness they pushed, but the land resisted, pressing them to the edges of the continent. For decades they roamed like thirsty men without a well, lacking even the means to convert the wild abundance to gold; for that, they needed people, processors, crafters, and manufacturers. So, they sent colonists, company men that could establish outposts and convert raw materials into saleable goods and, yes, continue the search for gold. The original Virginia colony, which was mapped to include nearly every known portion of the eastern coast, was established by the Virginia Company with the express purpose of mining gold and silver.

Colony life was hard. Harder, they never admitted back home, than such an abundance might have suggested. Just to survive the voyage was a triumph, to tame and claim the land after arrival, though, was what proved to be the real struggle. Early descriptions of the United Sates were filled with comparisons to hell. The men, promised easy money and an easier life in an abundant New World, fell apart, failing to maintain order and rebelling against their corporate and monarchical overseers. They were so far from home, surely those distant powers had no hold on them. Why work so hard for the benefit of someone else? Often, they didn't. In 1619 the Dutch decided to address this problem with forced labor, landing a boat of enslaved people on the continent. It was a gold mine, economically speaking, but settlements like Jamestown, filled with wild, unscrupulous, somewhat free men, still failed. Time passed. Ships came and went. Profits were made, but not a country.

It took the arrival of those with more resolute and righteous motives, the religious pilgrims who landed at Cape Cod, to establish a foothold, but by then, the spiritual hollow of slavery had already knitted itself to the American experience. Their small successes were hard earned. But unlike the commercial settlers, who had been lured by the promise of a life of leisure and easy riches, the pilgrims were at least prepared to face a wild place of biblical proportions. European propagandizers of the day, eager to entice potential settlers, had shifted tactics and started describing the New World not as a perfect, abundant paradise but as a wilderness that might become perfect, if only it were tamed. That taming, they said, could and should be done by righteous souls doing the good work of the Lord. It was a continuation of the creation myth in which, both Christian and Judaic traditions agree, the human race was granted dominion and stewardship over the natural world as a result of its descent from God. At its heart, this dominion cast humans as separate from the rest of nature.

This kind of thinking did more than motivate colonists to venture west. Once established, it encouraged them to assert individual dominion over the land by establishing ownership. They saw it as their destiny. To fulfill that destiny, colonists implemented a recognizable and quantifiable system of delineating space and establishing rights (their own) to land. An entire canon, impossible to adequately summarize here, exists on this issue and mindset, its authors ranging in scope and context from historical figures to modern historians, environmental and religious thinkers and philosophers, notable among them René Descartes, John Locke, Francis Bacon, Matthew Fox, Howard Zinn, William Cronon, Lynn White, Roderick Nash, and many others. One thing is consistent throughout, the relationship between the early colonists and the natural world would become a guiding system of beliefs that pervades the American mindset even today.

In the early days this belief system was driven by an important reality. Once in this New World, there was no going back. You survived, or you didn't. Even if they had the resources to turn back, to do so would have meant facing religious persecution or the same impoverished lives they had sought to escape. So motivated, they persisted, establishing homesteads, farming, and generally leaving their mark to prove their superiority over a land that ultimately was little more than a commercial construct—tilting at the windmill of the godless, wild, wilderness.

Never underestimate the power of a humble fence. Entire civilizations have been built on little more than a tenuous network of sticks or a linear stretch of carefully piled rocks. The whole of Christian Europe was a testament to this phenomenon. Ireland alone has more stone walls than any other place on Earth, perhaps in part due to its long history of conquest and seizure. Fences beget maps and maps are how you establish ownership. So, the colonists made maps. In these maps they documented their impact on and ownership of the land by assigning place names, delineating boundaries, and depicting what they saw as improvement and development, fences, roads, structures, wells, and gardens. In this way, they created something out of the perceived nothingness of the wild using the very same systems of social organization they came so far to escape.

For the most part, they relied on claiming a parcel of land, occupying it, and refusing to budge. It is an in-place way of being, to attach yourself to a particular parcel of land and stake your survival on it. But early Americans did it and did it well, manifesting a shared vision across the landscape: a fenced plot to call your own, a simple farmhouse; a grove of fruit trees in the front; behind, amber waves of grain. Paradise. The problem was, it was already being used.

For the Indigenous people who had inhabited the entirety of the continent for thousands of years, none of this made sense, especially the fences. These were, in a grossly broad comparison to the colonists, people who lived communal, seasonal, and transitory lifestyles. The utility of a fence or farmhouse in a way of life in which people and animals occupied broad swaths of overlapping and shifting territories, was difficult to imagine. Even those cultures that were known for their own developed uses of the land, like the Iroquois, held such vastly different notions of ownership, entitled use, and equity than the colonial settlers, that the colonists' mindset seemed, rightly, insane. These new people, with their strange ways of being were in the way. When neither kindness nor reason budged the settlers, conflict became inevitable.

Now the colonists had a moral quandary. They had claimed their land because of their belief that it wasn't being used and was in need of their stewardship. The clear and persistent evidence that it was, in fact, in use, and would require violence to keep, was problematic. You see, if the land was in use, then the pilgrim settlers, moralistic as they tended to be, couldn't claim it using either religious or legal precedents. If, in spite of the lack of fences or structures or tidy garden plots, it was in use, then according to their own logic, they didn't have any claim to be there at all. And yet, there they were, fences and all. With no place to go, the colonists dug in. The solution was not to radically change their way of life. It might have been, but it wasn't. They did not embrace communal living. They did not abandon their pastoral agrarian ways. They tore down no fences. What historian and environmental thinker William Cronon describes as fixity and good old-fashioned ideas of dominion won out. Instead, they assigned the same wildness they had been sold to motivate them to cross the Atlantic justify their claim to already occupied land. The initial cognitive leap was a small one, amounting to little more than a kind of medieval form of spiritual bypassing. The Indigenous people, living as they were seen by colonists, in among the wild things, seemingly free from puritanical mores, and praying, obviously, to a non-Christian god were clearly *of the wilderness.* It followed then, that the taming of the people of North America, was just as important and necessary a moral imperative as the seizure of its land. These people who existed outside the pale needed to be brought into the fold. Ultimately, the colonists were proposing little more than subjecting them to the same kinds of restrictions that had been imposed on them in Europe. History repeating.

But this was unbounded country. This was different. This othering, this commerce-driven enforcement of biblical dominion became a rabbit hole of inhumanity which would lead to the decimation and displacement of the people of North America. The pattern of migration, land claim, development, and conflict would quickly become a defining feature of the burgeoning American identity. One of the first things the United States government did upon the country gaining its independence was to establish an entirely new and uniquely American system of delineating space. That is to say, having won control over a large swath of land, they set about determining a new system of accounting for and ultimately partitioning it. It was a temper tantrum, really, an adolescent rejection of latitude and longitude that lay fixed on the prime meridian, centering the map on England. They called this new system township and range, and like most adolescent rebellions, it wasn't as unique as they thought. Like latitude and longitude, it used a series of vertical and horizontal lines across the map to create an ordered system of boxes. This new system divided the land area of the United States, which would someday exceed two billion acres, into surveyed parcels or "townships" that would, according to the Land Ordinance of 1785, be further surveyed, subdivided, and sold to white, male, citizens, the descendants of the original colonists and new European arrivals. Out of each township, they set aside a parcel that would reside in the public domain ensuring that the idea of government-owned and controlled land was normalized from the very beginning.

Two years later, realizing the need for western expansion to accommodate economic and population growth, they established the Northwest Ordinance, which set the procedure for newly mapped lands to become first territories and then states.

It also codified the notion that the United States and its people were entitled to those lands, regardless of their occupation by Indigenous groups. They were building on legal precedent set by colonial commercial powers. John Winthrop, the first governor of the Massachusetts Bay Colony had established settler rights to ownership of the land by having its wildness declared a legal vacuum. It was a tantalizing and simple concept and it was no wonder the idea made its way into early U.S. policy. By the time John Locke was writing about land ownership at the end of the fifteenth century, he was already using the word wilderness synonymously with "America." The new U.S. government was just codifying that belief. Once the land, or at least the map, was so codified, emigration west, and all that would come of it, was inevitable. Less than ten percent of the Indigenous people living in North America would survive it.

What would survive were the fences. Beyond them stretched seemingly endless boxes of township and range that reached farther and farther out across the map for more than two hundred years, eventually leading pilgrims in a procession of wagons to a low rise in the dusty desert, still searching for that promised land.

SIGNPOST

The occupation of the American West was accomplished along trails that were often little more than scratches in the dirt. The experience of that migration, especially those first tragic years, has become for the American people one of the "every man." It exists in our collective experience as a shared struggle that helps define us as a whole. While our journey in this volume is through Oregon Country, it starts in a shapeless desert wash some two hundred miles to the east of Oregon. The Humboldt Sink in Nevada was the beginning of the emigrant experience of the Applegate Trail, even though the Applegates themselves scouted the road from the opposite direction. To know the experience of the Sink, then, is to know something of the people who traveled the road. It could have been any of us.

TWO

TRAIL STORY: NORTH TO TREES, SOUTH TO GOLD

"Sunday, July 15. —A march of five hours brought us to the vicinity of the Sink of Humboldt River, at about nine o'clock: and continuing over a well-beaten sandy trail until noon, we encamped on the edge of the Great Desert. Of late the region through which we journey had been growing more and more desolate; but here was reached what might be aptly termed 'the valley of the shadow of death,' and over its portals might be inscribed: 'Who enters here, leaves hope behind.'

—WILLIAM G. JOHNSTON, 1849

Most of the wagons had oxen. For those making the entire 2,500-mile trip from Missouri to the west coast, they were preferred. Horses weren't strong enough to pull the nearly two-thousand-pound loads each wagon would carry. Mules were easily stolen. Oxen were tough to the point of mean, though when yoked together, still easy enough to prod forward with little more than a hand whip, stick, and loud voice. But they turned the wagons into giant sloth, creeping across the central plains and over the rumpled ridgelines of the Rocky Mountains at about two miles an hour.

At that pace, even the women and children could keep up on foot, which was good, because every inch of every wagon was loaded down with provisions, even after several months on the trail. There wasn't any room for seats.

They had tools, mostly, and raw materials, rather than actual possessions. They had nails, fabric, medicines, food, guns, and ammunition, things for survival on the trail and upon arrival, wherever and whenever that may be. Most of what they needed, sometimes even the most basic of things like blankets, they made as they went along or traded for with Indigenous people and trappers. But still the wagons spilled over, and the oxen strained against the weight. The white-bonnet covers, swaying and billowing as the wagons rumbled bobbed and floated like, it was said, schooners on the sea. In practice, that image dissolved as a mirage. The wagons were lumbering behemoths. And heavy. Everything that could be double-packed was: winter clothing was wrapped around anything breakable while bacon and other perishable food was packed inside grain sacks to keep them cool. What they couldn't fit inside was tied on; washbasins and jockey boxes clung to the sides of the bed; a bucket of tar and tallow used to lubricate the wheels dangled from the back. Those wagons were everything. Aside from shelter and storage, good wagons were designed to be converted to boats for larger river crossings. A good wagon would save your life many times.

There weren't seats in the wagons, but if there had been, they would never have been used. Someone had to herd the rest of the food, the goats and pigs, the milk cows and calves, along the trail, besides, the ride was painfully rough. So, they walked.

They walked past St. Louis, out of the United States, across the great plains, up, over the high peaks and folds of the Rocky Mountains, and into the high deserts of the Western Cordilleran region. They walked through waist-high prairie grass in places so flat for so far you could practically see the curvature of the earth and over loose rock and packed ice in high passes. They walked in summer sun and under storms. They walked. Sometimes they walked while carrying a baby on one arm, other times pulling an obstinate animal, each day bleeding into the next except for the gradual change of the landscape and the position of the sun in the sky. Some attached wooden odometers, made with simple cogs and gears, to their wagon wheels to track their progress. Others just pressed west, as far as they could, every day.

There was never any shade. Weeks turned to months under the trail's full sun. It seemed impossible that anyplace could cast less shadows than the flats of the prairies, but the salt flats and sandy basins that greeted the travelers in what would become Nevada managed it. The canvas wagon covers, always in plain white, offered little respite even after the drawstrings were pulled tight over the hickory frame.

By the time they reached the Humboldt Sink, the cattle were nearly dead.

The Sink, the western edge of what was called the "forty-mile desert," was a sandy stretch of heat and blinding light on the westernmost edge of the Great Basin. The land in the region, which extends from eastern Utah to the foothills of the Sierra Nevada Mountains in California, is being slowly stretched by tectonic forces. The result of this extension of the earth's crust is a topography characterized by long, squat ranges and flat-bottomed valleys trending north-south, against the directional pull. The effect from an aerial view is one of stretch marks. To someone traveling such a landscape by foot, it might appear that one has crossed the same ridge over and over again, always to find another sandy basin reaching out to the north and south, always another ridge ahead to the west. Ridges and valleys, ridges and valleys.

The sun passing overhead was perhaps the defining feature of the landscape and definitely the determiner of most things. In such places, plants, animals, and humans all live and die on its terms. It has been like this for eons. Over the past 13,000 years, its condition has trended toward heat and desiccation. First, it receded the massive sheet of glacial ice that had progressed from the north in the last ice age; then it went after the water, filling and emptying the basins of the region in time to its own internal rhythms. In the past few hundred years, rapid warming has tipped the hydrologic balance, leaving vast stretches of salt and mudflats where lakes once sat. Some of these, like the Humboldt Sink, still catch enough water from their surrounding watersheds to, on the wettest of years, fill some portion of the basins with shallow lakes. At times, they can stretch to more than thirty or forty square miles in area. Some years they are completely dry.

Lacking reliable rain or groundwater, they empty quickly, even though as a rule, they are terminal—these basins were created by tectonic rather than surface erosion processes and so possess no natural outlet. The water simply evaporates away.

It makes for thirsty country. In the forty-mile desert, the sun shines, most would say beats down, the majority of days. Average summertime temperatures can be well in excess of one hundred degrees Fahrenheit, hot enough to cause the white salts and buff sands to reradiate the heat, bending the light back up again as heat waves and mirages. Because the rate of evaporation exceeds the rate at which fresh water is able to dilute the salts contributed by the surrounding country rock, what water *is* in the Sink is always saline.

Eventually, even the air dries out, and once the sun does go down, nighttime temperatures, unmodulated by humidity, plunge, often thirty to forty degrees overnight. It is a phenomenon that has a particularly pronounced effect on human physiology, especially when paired with exhaustion or sunburn. Hypothermia and frostbite are common in the desert at night, where temperatures can drop below zero even in summer. Freeze-free days in the area of the Humboldt Sink number fewer than seventy per year. Dust storms are frequent. And if by chance it does rain, even miles in the distance, drainage channels might swell so quickly with water that smaller mules and sheep could be swept away.

Under such conditions everything, even the ground, is desperate. One emigrant, Elisha Perkins wrote of thc place in 1849 saying, "Here we see our last of the famous Humboldt.... The stream itself does not deserve the name of river being only a good-sized creek.... For the first two day's travel in its valley, the grass is splendid, then the valley begins to narrow & feed to get poorer & less of it all the rest of its course, till for the last 80 miles except in special spots we could hardly get enough for our mules to eat, & water barely drinkable from saline & sulphurous impregnation & having a milky color. I think Baron Humboldt would feel but littlc honored by his name being affixed to a stream of so little pretension." But perhaps Mr. J. Quinn Thorton put it most eloquently, "...it was as the River of Death dried up.... The [e]arth appeared to be as destitute of moisture, as if a drop of rain or dew had never fallen upon it from the brazen heavens above." Survival, for those who remain determined, is possible.

Contrary to what emigrant diaries may suggest, the area has a long history of, if not occupation, successful use, by humans. Indigenous Americans from several periods and groups hunted and fished the Humboldt Sink, taking advantage of the abundance of waterfowl and migratory birds that used the lake when it was present. Canada geese reside there in large numbers, feeding on pondweed. So do American coots, in astonishing numbers; some flocks exceed 100,000 members. Along with them are teals and pintails and an assortment of other smaller ducks. Farther upland, California quail root for bugs among the scrub brush and Mule deer linger near dense stands of willow. Predators and scavengers, bobcats and kit foxes, beaver, muskrat, and mink also make their way, drawn by the promise of water.

In truth, the pioneers, ignorant regarding the abundance of potential food sources and motivated as they were by the promise of water, resembled wild animals. Most arrived to the driest portions of the trail in the heat of August. If lucky, they would be able to leapfrog through the desert using its network of springs. By then, the wagon train would have stretched out into distinct clumps several dozen prairie schooners, sometimes with days or weeks between them, as ability, illness, and misfortune held them back. Often, they traveled the desert at night, moving from freshwater spring to freshwater spring by moonlight in the frigid cold. Not every spring appeared as promised. Some years, water in the region was so scarce it was common to find hand-dug wells clogged with dead livestock, buzzards circling overhead in the heat. The water from these clay holes was murky. Some produced water so hot the women could wash clothing in them, one of the few amenities afforded by the land. Even so, men reported being able to drink it up faster than it ran out of the ground.

History would lead us to believe that only men made the journey west. Certainly, they were the only ones to be allowed to claim land, own businesses, or write laws. But the truth is that the travelers, for the most part, were family groups, often several brothers or cousins along with their wives and, typically, abundant numbers of children. The men, mostly young, were well-armed and worn-shoed, carrying knives at their chests or waists, rifles and water across their backs. The wide brims of their hats extended nearly past their lean shoulders, which were draped with simple shirts tucked into sturdy pants, suspenders holding the two together. They wore beards with no moustache hung low off chins, or thick, handlebar mustaches, twisted at the ends or shaved into a steep, overturned U. They drove the oxen, hunted and fished, scouted the route for obstacles and safety, tended to the animals, forded rivers, and fixed wagons along with anything else that needed fixing.

Women on the trail were ghosts. They traveled covered from their chins to their ankles and wrists in fabric. Layers of thick skirts and aprons and wide-brimmed bonnets that covered their faces ensured they were well shielded from sun and man. Physical modesty, mostly neglected among men, was considered crucial for women. But in such conditions, it was hard to come by. If other women were in the company, they could rely on one another to shield themselves on the open prairie. If alone, they relied on the abundance of their skirts. But that is where the utility of their dress ended. Sometimes, even that could prove fatal, their long woolen skirts were prone to catching in wagon wheels or alighting in campfires.

In daily life and on the trail, the women were looked down upon as dependents or even hindrances, but they were necessary for survival. To begin with, women were essential for ambitious men with a hunger for land. Having a wife got you 640 acres in claim, twice the amount of land allowed for a single man. And women worked, even on the trail. They cooked, fed and herded animals, mended clothing, and crafted soaps, candles, and other necessities, all while nursing, cleaning, and caring for children. They served other male purposes as well. More often than not, they were pregnant for at least some portion of the journey.

While journals and letters of woman-pioneers rarely discuss issues of the body or pregnancies, births on the trail were frequent, and those dates were duly noted. The long days, the walking, and the lack of sanitation conspired to increase infant and maternal mortality rates. The wagon trains, immersed as they were in gold fever, did not slow for recovery, and the solitary nature of the journey for many of these women did not help. In groups they could act as nurses and doulas, but most often, they were on their own.

The children held a another, particularly tenuous position. Death, especially of infants, was heartbreakingly common. Conversely, it was common for children to survive when their parents did not, leaving them orphaned in empty country. In those cases, they were taken up as wards by whomever felt up to the task of getting them...anywhere but the Sink.

Where does one go from such a place of death and desperation? That choice would come as soon as they had taken what water and rest they could and the first team of oxen was pushed back onto the trail. There, just beyond the Sink, following a big bend in the Humboldt River, the trail diverged, it is said, at a sandy rise marked by a red barrel with a square hole cut in its top, the exterior painted red but fading quickly in the sun; an emigrant's postbox of which there were many scattered along the trail. Such boxes were typically filled with letters, journals, and notes of advice and adorned with advertisements, enticements, and warnings. At the Sink, all the contents regarded a single choice, which all who arrived at that point now faced: north to trees, or south to gold.

THREE

THE SOIL AND FACE OF THE COUNTRY, 1800–1840

AT THE BEGINNING OF THE 1800S, THE TIDY SQUARES OF THE township and range system stretched west across the map until they disappeared about a third of the way across the continent like a Cheshire cat into a vast uncharted territory that was not yet claimed by the United States. And for the most part, Americans didn't really mind. They had spent the previous fifty years fighting alternately for survival and independence and, having achieved some measure of both, now set about the task of establishing themselves as part of a new great, modern nation. It was no small task. They had an entire society to invent and the unknown lands west may well have been across the ocean for their distance. In spite of this casual disregard, the rest of the continent, the Pacific Northwest and what was then Spanish-occupied northern Mexico, was still locked in the battle for survival and self-governance. The United States, still railing against Great Britain, sided with Spain and France. When France prevailed, it took its lesson from history and did not attempt to build a new country so far from the homeland. And so, the United States was practically gifted the middle of the continent in the Louisiana Purchase of 1803. Suddenly, the United States was one of the largest countries in the world, in possession of 530 million new acres of land, at the bargain price of just four cents an acre.

President Thomas Jefferson believed that the American Dream, the American destiny, lay in that land to the west. He seized on the moment, riding a wave of supportive nationalism to turn the population's eyes to the western frontier and capture their imaginations. A brave new world was waiting to be built in that vast country and prosperity was sure to follow. More than that, those lands, he believed, promised adventure and a life of unfettered freedom. Americans believed him.

There was also a new kind of revolution at hand. The innovations of the early industrial revolution had inspired a sense of possibility that proved more powerful and motivating than the moral imperatives and struggle for survival that had consumed early Americans. As a result, a new era of curiosity and critical thought was opening. Now, along with their thirst for land and freedom, the American public was thirsty for scientific knowledge and understanding. It was in abundance. New scientific instruments and tools were being invented all the time, looms, and batteries, and something they were calling a steam engine was in the works. Even the number of clocks in homes was increasing.

Surveying, with all its gadgets and measurements, was suddenly an esteemed profession, especially as the still-young country invested in large-scale infrastructure projects like railroads, canals, and roadways. It was a global phenomenon. For the first time, entire countries were being mapped in detail, providing, finally, clear pictures of terrain, passages, and political boundaries. Notable among these endeavors was the Great Trigonometric Survey of India, which not only mapped the Himalayan Mountains but also provided one of the first accurate measurements of a longitudinal arc. Around the world mapping was embraced as a show of political prowess. The United States, eager to establish itself on the world stage, also set about quantifying itself, especially through land surveys. The wilderness to the west, for so long the house of the ungodly and the unknown, became a thing of quantifiable fascination.

Meanwhile, the increased global reliance on whaling had created crowded seas. Now though, the men who set out across the oceans were more than adventurous capitalists seeking trade routes and gold. There was now a global trade of knowledge in addition to goods. So included among the old-world sailors, swashbucklers, soldiers, traders, and human traffickers were great thinkers and observers of the natural world, men who were driven by a sense of curiosity and scientific inquiry.

One of them, Alexander von Humboldt, would come to have his name splashed across maps of the western United States without ever setting foot in any of the country that would bear his name. He was Prussian, born in 1769, and a geologist by education and trade. He spent his early career working as a mine inspector in the Bayreuth and the Fichtel Mountains, where he oversaw massive increases in gold production. There, he began to establish his own unique views on science, humanity, and the ethics of both which he put to good use by establishing a relief fund for mine workers that had suffered illness or injury from the hazardous conditions.

Later, he worked as a cartographer. He was good at it, and his detailed and accurate work came to be relied upon by mapmakers around the world. He spent five years at the turn of the eighteenth century exploring and describing central and south America and spent a large portion of that time in Mexico. He was a keen collector of specimen and samples, a careful and detailed observer, known for his love of instrumentation and measurement. As Humboldt traveled, he practiced his own bespoke kind of science, integrating the brand-new fields of meteorology, natural history, geology, and biology with mathematics and romantic philosophy. As a result, he was the first person to record and describe changes in weather patterns, plant life, and other natural indicators that what would come to be known as human-induced climate change, a phenomenon he tracked for more than thirty years. Eventually, he used this vast collection of lived scientific experience and knowledge of the world to derive what he saw as a unifying theory. He called it Kosmos, from the ancient Greek *cosmos*. In Kosmos, he described the universe as an ordered complex system that existed in opposition to chaos and of which humans, and all other things, were an integral, and equally important, part.

It was as much a radical idea for its time as it is now, in no small part for its rejection of biblical conceptions of time and beliefs about creation and dominion in the natural world. In Humboldt's universe, humans were part of, not above the natural world. While his ideas pushed back against those long-standing religious perspectives on humanity's role as elevated stewards of the Earth, his philosophy as a whole was widely accepted, especially by Americans. And why not? His time in the Americas had been integral to his development of Kosmos about which he said, "It was the discovery of America that planted the seed of the Kosmos." Still, he visited the United States just twice, in large part because of its attachment to slavery, which he accurately called "devilish."

Humboldt's views on slavery didn't prevent him from meeting with President Jefferson, whose own interest in science, exploration, and natural history was well known. In 1804 Jefferson had already organized the Lewis and Clark Expedition when Humboldt wrote to him from Cuba saying he could detour to the United States. Jefferson jumped at the chance. He had just completed the Louisiana Purchase and desperately needed to fill in the map. He hoped Humboldt could provide him with information about Spanish-occupied portions of northern Mexico, with which the United States now shared a hazily drawn border. Humboldt could indeed, and he provided many more details to fill in the map, including information on climate, terrain, and population. Jefferson would later refer to Humboldt as "the most scientific man of the age."

So armed, Jefferson launched the Corps of Discovery later that same year. The overarching goal, and the one that had secured funding for the expedition, was to find boat passage to the Pacific, the Northwest Passage—the same trade route that colonial explorers had searched for nearly two hundred years earlier. Led by Meriwether Lewis and William Clark, the Corps' other mission was to survey the land acquired in the Louisiana Purchase and add shape to the somewhat undefined south and western boundaries of the agreement, to describe, as Jefferson put it in his written instructions to them, "the soil and face of the country." That goal made them more than pathfinders, they would also be surveyors, botanists, and ambassadors charged with taking the first steps to fulfilling their country's sense of "Manifest Destiny": the belief that it was the destiny of the United States to occupy and control all the land from the Atlantic to the Pacific.

They were progressive for their time. Uninterested in the old colonial rhetoric of savage wilderness or the settler practice of erasure and displacement, the Corps of Discovery set about documenting the people who inhabited the West in the hopes that Americans could integrate with them. It wouldn't work. The U.S. population increased from 5 million in 1800 to 13 million by 1830, crowding eastern cities. Western lands, not all of which were even considered U.S. territory began to hold appeal. But there was, still, that old issue of use. Much of those western lands were clearly occupied by Indigenous people and too much time had passed to ignore the issue with magical, biblical thinking. But something had to be done. The dilemma was addressed in the passage of the Indian Removal Act which empowered the government to begin the process of purchasing or trading Indian land through treaties.

America pushed west.

The Corps of Discovery found no Northwest Passage. So those who made their way to the Pacific Northwest in the first quarter of the century arrived the long way round by sea, or overland by foot. They were trappers and hunters, mountain men, as they would come to be known and they relied on grit and their wits to traverse the landscape. Most of the route to the Northwest was still unmapped, and those famous wagon ruts were not yet carved into the land. Navigation by bearing and stars was still important, but not nearly as much so as the extensive network of trails established by Indigenous people, who still numbered in the hundreds of thousands. The mountain men hunted beaver and traded with these people and used their trade routes to forge and codify their own inroads.

Among them were Jedediah Smith, John Jacob Aster, and Peter Skene Ogden. As a whole they were almost universally sent by the Hudson's Bay Company or invested colonial powers with a singular purpose: servicing the fur trade. Though they are credited with being the first to "settle" the land, these men lived lives of rough subsistence, often traveling continuously or, conversely, sheltering in place for months at a time. The mountain men dressed in animal hides and wore coonskin caps. They faced off with grizzly bears and wolves and, it was said, pulled fish straight out of the streams with their bare hands. They lived solitary lives, devoid of sophistication or refinement.

Even so, these rough around the edges mountain men became an important trope for the American people, cementing in their minds the stereotypes of masculinity and self-reliance as inherent to the fabric of the American landscape, even if the mountain men weren't all, or even predominately, American. It was an irony.

In contrast to the isolation and primitive nature of the mountain men's existence, the Indigenous cultures which were being displaced had sophisticated cultures and developed uses of the western lands they occupied, including agriculture and commerce. They worked the land, erecting complexly engineered fishing dams and platforms and managing controlled wildfires They were far more adept at surviving—and thriving—than the mountain men, and they did so while including and even venerating women and children. And they were sophisticated in other ways. They had a rich tradition of the aesthetic arts, with music, dance, and basketry and woodcarving all held in high esteem and a long tradition of their own kind of scientific observations and insights. But those were not the stories that were told about them back east to a population still willfully clinging to stories of disuse and savagery. Instead, tall tales of adventure by solitary, masculine heroes were fed to the masses. The mountain man had become a new American ideal.

Not all mountain men fit the legends. Some broke the stereotype and continued on the progressive and scientific path carved out by Humboldt and Lewis and Clark before them. Peter Skene Ogden described the vegetation, fish, and wildlife of southern Oregon. David Douglas was a botanist and traveled with the Hudson's Bay Company. He described much of the ecology of the northwest, including its iconic pines, which now bear his name. But most just sent back as many beaver and fox and other pelts as they could. And they did so with an increasing urgency.

As the United States looked to fulfill its Manifest Destiny and accommodate the demands of its growing population, it was encroaching on territory still claimed by France, Spain, and England. The environment paid a heavy price for the conflict. The beaver ended up being trapped nearly to extinction, not because of too many fancy easterners wearing fur coats, but as a means of weaponization. The European countries, so far away, reasoned that if they hunted the beaver, until then the only real monetized resource to emerge from the region, to extinction, there would be no cause for America to push west beyond the confines of the Louisiana Purchase. If the land remained largely unoccupied by settlers, they postulated, they could maintain possession by default. It was an environmental catastrophe. The loss of the beaver, nature's hydrologists, had a massive and immediate impact on the surface of the land. Ponds overtopped and spillways appeared, erosion and flooding changed places, entire fishing areas were lost. And that wasn't all, the mountain men had introduced new microorganisms, like smallpox, to the environment, changing the balance of the ecosystem and causing devastation in the Indigenous population disproportionate to their actual numbers.

To the east, neither loss resonated. Too far from anyone or anything, the events to the west may well have been taking place on the moon. Besides, slavery, the ongoing dehumanization of people based on unsubstantiated scientific claims, prohibited a compassionate response to the news. Two hundred years of forced labor and urban development had taken their toll on American humanity and removed them from their connection to the natural world. To many Americans it had been so long since the eastern seaboard had been a wilderness, one could hardly picture such a place in one's mind. In 1840 historian and philosopher Alexis de Tocqueville described the growing disconnection from the wilderness: "Americans themselves hardly give it a thought. The wonders of inanimate nature leave them cold, and it is hardly an exaggeration to say that they do not see the admirable forests that surround them until the trees fall to their axes."

All of that began to change when a new group of revolutionary thinkers, artists, and activists, inspired by Humboldt some fifty years after his voyages to the Americas, redefined the American relationship to the wild. Among them were scientists like Charles Darwin, who brought Humboldt's early works with him aboard the *Beagle* in the 1830s; writers and philosophers such as Ralph Waldo Emerson (*Nature*), Henry David Thoreau (*Walden*), and Walt Whitman (*Leaves of Grass*) who were inspired and guided by Humboldt's Kosmos; and artists, most especially the members of the Hudson School, a group of painters including Frederic Church and his contemporaries.

These men, and the few women they included in their ranks, paleontologist Mary Anning, journalist Margaret Fuller, and painters Susie M. Barstow and Harriet Cany, among them, revered and memorialized the American landscape by quantified and detailed observation, defining the soil and face of the country in terms of both beauty, spirit, and science. Taken together, their work created a narrative of the land not so different from the early colonial propaganda and often deeply connected to matters of the human soul, but firmly rooted in reason and scientific thought. But by then, freedom of religion seekers and religious radicals, another product of the enlightenment, were already pushing west. All that was still to come, but it would be missionaries, not scientists, who settled Oregon.

SIGNPOST

The Applegate Trail and the trials of the Humboldt Sink were not the first emigrant trail experience. The original Oregon Trail was a more than 2,000-mile route that connected the Missouri River with the Willamette Valley in Oregon. The journey was dangerous and death was common, most often through disease, accident, or violence. While no official death count exists, it is estimated that of the more than 400,000 people who attempted the journey, at least 20,000 died. The Applegate brothers and their families were among the first to make the journey.

FOUR

TRAIL STORY: SEEING THE ELEPHANT

"Dear Brother, I will start with my family to Oregon Ty [Territory], this spring Lindsay and perhaps Charles will go with me. This resolution has been conceived and matured in a very short time, but it is probably destiny, to which account I place it having neither time nor good reasons to offer in defense of so wild an undertaking...."

—JESSE APPLEGATE, APRIL, 11, 1843

IN 1831, THE STORY GOES, A PAIR OF NEZ PERCE INDIANS arrived in St. Louis asking about a book called the Bible and "white man's heaven." The news inspired a surge of missionary fervor, most particularly in a young Methodist minister by the name of Marcus Whitman, who set out west with his wife, Narcissa, in one of the very first settlement groups, to travel what would become the Oregon Trail and build a life in what was not yet the United States.

Twenty-eight-year-old Narcissa hated it from the very first moment, complaining in her diary of the hard life on the trail, the dust and heat, the boredom and the "savage Indians" for which she held clear disdain for. "Never was I more keenly sensible to the self-denials of a missionary life," she wrote. "Even now while I am writing, the drum and the savage yell are sounding in my ears, every sound of which is as far as the east is from the west from vibrating in unison with my feelings...Dear friends, will you not sometime think of me almost alone in the midst of savage darkness."

The trip was hard and slow, so hard that until then the mountain men had insisted it was impossible for women to make it successfully. The Whitmans got as far as Walla Walla, at the intersection of what would become Oregon, Washington, and Idaho. There, they joined forces with another missionary couple to build a wooden fort along the Columbia River. Then they turned to the business of finding and converting those supposedly Bible-curious Indians.

Unsurprisingly, the story proved untrue. The Indigenous people were not having it. Who were these ranting white men and their hateful-looking women? They didn't bother to inquire further, instead launching a series of attacks on the mission. The message was clear: go home. But Whitman was not deterred. In addition to his religious mission, he was an expansionist. In his eyes, the problem was not that they were unwanted or unneeded, but that they were outnumbered. After several years of failed attempts, he resolved to travel east to bring more people, more *Americans*, to Oregon Territory—even if he had to go there and drag them back himself.

By 1840 it seemed like the whole world was moving to St. Louis. And why not? It had theater, music, dance halls, a thriving waterfront scene, and even, recently, a public school system. Positioned on the western edge of the frontier, disputed territory notwithstanding, it had been a bustling port city and center of trade for as long as anyone could remember and before that. Indigenous North Americans had long used its location just south of the confluence of the Missouri and Mississippi rivers as a meeting place and cultural center. In the late 1700s and early 1800s Voyageurs, French men who worked the fur trade, and the Hudson's Bay Company's mountain men used it as their own trading post. By the mid-1800s, commerce, agriculture, and other industries had arrived, providing plenty of opportunities for new immigrants who were being squeezed out of crowded eastern cities. Many were German and Irish who had fled to America to escape famine and war, most were young men with families looking for honest work, but there were also prospectors of all kinds, drawn by the promises of the opening west.

The influx of arrivals brought increased competition and saturated markets. Then, when the depression that had been brewing to the east finally hit the frontier in 1839, the local economy collapsed. Suddenly, everyone was pinched as the price of production outpaced market prices. It got so bad that at one point they had to sell off bacon for less than the price of the salt used to cure it.

The Applegates—Charles, Lindsay, and Jesse—were three of five brothers born in Kentucky and raised in Illinois farm country. Longing for elbow room and in need of affordable land to start their own farms and families, they moved to Missouri in the 1830s. Charles and Lindsay were farmers, and Lindsay ran a successful mill operation. Jesse, the youngest of the three, had attended Rock Spring Seminary to study surveying but had aspirations that leaned toward adventure. And there was plenty of adventure calling. Previously Jesse had been a trapper, and a friend of his had been a member of Aster's trapping expedition to Oregon Territory. The prospect of such country excited him, but after he was unable to find employment with the fur companies, he resolved to settle down. He found work as a surveyor plotting out parcels and got himself a small farm near his brothers', which he worked with his wife, Cynthia, and baby girl, their first child. They could grow their operations slowly over time. St. Louis County, surely, would never fill up.

But the people kept coming. All along the Mississippi River new cities and industries were appearing. In the 1840s, St. Louis started to suffer growing pains due to its ballooning population and, increasingly, ideological issues. Missouri was a slave state, but St. Louis was filled with people from all over the country, not all of whom agreed with the practice. Conflict over the issue was becoming inevitable. The Applegate brothers, perhaps influenced by a young, but already influential politician in Illinois, Abraham Lincoln, were vehemently opposed to the practice. Unable to either tolerate or convince their neighbors to change their ways, and in search of economic opportunity, they once again looked to move on. Someplace west, perhaps. Jesse had his eye on Oregon Country. St. Louis had been a launching place for travelers destined for the Oregon Territory ever since Lewis and Clark had begun their Corps of Discovery expedition from its banks in 1804.

That expedition failed to find the passage but had managed to captivate the imaginations of young, midcentury men like the Applegate brothers, drawing them to the edge of the frontier. Like many of their cohort, they had grown up hearing stories of the heroism and struggles the Corps faced and the harsh conditions they endured. At one point, the older boys would tell them, they even had to devour their candles to survive. It was not considered a journey for family men, meaning it wasn't considered a journey for women. By 1840, the few early wagons that had managed by some miracle to survive the journey had a name for facing down the worst of what the trail had to offer and surviving; they called it "seeing the elephant," a colonial term used to describe a sudden and disheartening fall from excitement into disenchantment, fear, and catastrophe such as when an encounter with a wild animal goes awry.

Recognizing that trial and hardship do little to entice customers, advertisers and promoters latched onto the romanticism created by the Corps, not the brutal realities being experienced by groups like the Whitmans. Eager to make money off the opening west, they pushed the prospect of a new life in a land of abundance—and their goods and services in aid of getting there to St. Louis's public. In Oregon, these promoters would tell you, life was easy: Trees so tall you couldn't see their tops nearly jumped out of the ground when they saw an ax, fish leaped right out of the water and into the pan, and fully cooked pigs ran wild through the forest, forks already sticking out from their sides. You had to see it for yourself, they told the young men who gathered around to listen. You have to see it yourself.

Jesse Applegate was one of the believers. It helped that bolstering the claims was a good friend, Robert Shortess, who had emigrated to Oregon Country in 1840. Ever since, he had sent back a steady stream of letters describing the abundant trees, fish-filled rivers, and rich soils of the Willamette Valley, though sorely, no roasted pigs. More importantly, his friend wrote to Jesse, there was talk of statehood. Shortess himself was helping to craft the provisional government. If only he would make the trip, Jesse could play a role in the new government.

Losing more money than he was making, Jesse became resolved. He started working on his brothers. They too, were facing hard times, and the prospect of the journey and later settling in the company of their brothers, Jesse thought, would surely be appealing. He was right.

In 1843, the Applegate brothers sold their farms and headed out west in search of independence, prosperity, and influence. They planned to follow the lead of Whitman, who, having decided that he did indeed need to drag new settlers out personally, had kept the violent opposition of the Indigenous people to himself. The brothers invested in wagons and provisions and purchased several hundred head of cattle, which they planned to drive along with them to Oregon. Then the brothers and their families, a party of twenty-seven, joined a large train of at least one hundred wagons and nearly one thousand people that they themselves had helped rouse by placing an ad about the trip in the *Bonneville Herald*. It was the first large-scale emigration wagon train of its kind.

The Applegates and their party had no presidential directive or noble quest to bind them to one another. With little experience, high stakes, and many unknowns, tempers frayed easily. It took just days for Peter Burnett, a failed merchant and debtor initially elected to lead the caravan, to lose his position over a botched river crossing and ineffective leadership.

It went downhill from there. Without clear leadership and under pressure to cross the mountains ahead of winter weather in the western mountains, the train broke into two parties. Those who were slow moving or traveling with large herds of livestock fell behind to form their own company called the 'Cow Column.' They elected Jesse Applegate to lead them.

It proved a good choice. In comparison to the diaries and letters of later emigrants, the group's trip across the plains and over the Rockies was uncharacteristically easy. Jesse brought order and discipline to the Cow Column. Each day followed a predictable schedule and the emigrant's positions in the train was consistently rotated, ensuring that no one party "eat another's dust" too long. In his diary, Jesse, describes his method of maintaining order writing, "All know when, at 7 O'clock, the signal to march sounds that those not ready to take their proper places in the line of march must fall into the dusty rear for the day." The days were long, usually beginning at 4 a.m. with a wakeup call of shots firing, but the food was plenty (pork and flapjacks for breakfast, buffalo or other game for dinner) and at night there was music around the fire. People got along. Having followed missionary Marcus Whitman, they successfully arrived at his fort in Walla Walla at the bank of the Columbia River in October of 1843. It was just weeks before the start of winter. Fort Walla Walla was a significant milestone of the journey, a place where the dry, grassy flatlands and vast prairie finally began to give way to the Ponderosa pines that signaled entry to alpine country. The final push west would lead them over the high peaks of the Cascade Mountains. Still active volcanoes, the Cascades were an untidy row of overlapping mountains covered within dense temperate forests dominated by massive Douglas fir trees that blocked passage and obscured sightlines. Word was, it was hard going, especially with wagons. Lewis and Clark, and nearly everyone else since, had avoided those mountains, opting instead to run the massive Columbia River.

At Walla Walla, the train disbanded as each family chose their own paths, setting off to make their way to their personal promised lands and their own western stories. Some headed north to trapping country, others decided to forgo the mountains, settling in the high desert cattle country of the east. Some chose to find a place to over winter, waiting for the following spring to make their way into the western valleys. Some, like the Applegates, would race the coming winter and continue west, taking the river route. Most of those that opted to take the river did so haphazardly, lashing together logs as makeshift rafts and piling them so high with provisions and possessions that they sank low into the fast-moving water. Being of some means, the Applegate brothers could afford to pay to send their animals overland while the families floated the river. They stayed near Walla Walla for several weeks to hire a river guide and construct proper boats. In St. Louis, they'd spent some time on the water and felt they were well-suited for the river run. Besides, most of the trip was supposed to be on smooth waters. Before they reached those smooth waters though, they had to navigate a rocky, rapids-filled, six-mile-long portion of the river that led to an Indigenous trading post and seasonal fishing village called The Dalles.

The segment of river leading to The Dalles was notorious for its whirlpools, side channels, and waterfalls, some of which, like Celilo Falls, were developed with fishing platforms that extended over the surface of the falling water. In places, large, building-sized blocks of basalt, remnants of the Columbia River flood basalts, stuck out of the water. Many considered the stretch too dangerous to navigate and chose to walk the banks carrying their supplies and boats with them. Even Lewis and Clark had portaged this portion of the river when they arrived in the region.

Eager to find shelter in the valley before winter, the Applegates didn't have time for a portage. They decided to make the run. It was a decision that would make their first taste of Oregon

Country bitter. They set off from the north side of the river on November 4. They were a group of about sixty, distributed across several mackinaws, wide, flat-bottomed boats that resemble oversized canoes with sails. They were more stable and faster than rafts. It took them several days to reach The Dalles rapids, towards which the group reported traveling largely without worry. Staid and grim-faced, the brothers were known for their even-handed leadership and midwestern stoicism. Unlike many pioneers, the Applegate brothers were not superstitious men, but the women in the family perhaps were. Subsequent generations of Applegates have recounted an incident in those first days along the river which hints at the mystical. On that occasion, family lore recounts, Jesse's wife, Cynthia, perhaps agitated by a passing raven, prophesized an impending death in the company. The journey had been long and hard and everyone was tired, so her warning was dismissed. The brothers had their own concerns about timing, money, and what lay ahead. The upcoming river rapids at the Dalles too, had them worried, as they found themselves feeling uneasy in the hands of their guide, a local Indigenous man with whom they were barely able to communicate.

Days later, they made the run. The first boats did well, but one of the later boats was pulled into a strong current near the south shore and went down. In the boat was Alexander McClellan, a seventy-year-old friend of the family they all called Uncle Mac, Cynthia's twenty-one-year-old brother William Parker and four young boys: Billy Doak, a family friend, Elisha and Warren, Lindsay's sons, and Edward, Jesse's boy. When the boat capsized in the whirlpool, everyone was thrown into the water. Those that were strong swimmers fared well. William made it safely to shore. Elisha swam to one of the basalt outcrops in the river towing Billy, who stayed above the water by holding onto a tick, a kind of makeshift mattress that was little more than a sack of feathers. Uncle Mac was last seen trying to keep little Edward's head above the water. No one seems to have seen what happened to Warren. Already safely down shore, the rest of the Applegates could only watch. Grief hit them like a wave and immediately sought an outlet, first at their guide, whose own boat had safely navigated the run and then at the Indigenous people gathered along the shore who they would later claim had not attempted a rescue. Surely the river was not to blame; a loss of so much life must be someone's fault and these were the only people close at hand.

Susan Applegate, a direct descendant of the brothers and steward of the family's stories, describes their reactive and prejudiced thinking, and the role of the river in the tragedy this way:

> *"Jesse's and Lindsay's sons died in a capsized boat. But there again, you know, when the boat was coming down the river, there were three of them, mackinaws they made from driftwood and all their belongings and the three boys were in one and an old man who was a family friend.... When the boys drowned Lindsay thought that maybe the Indians had tricked them, that this was a purposeful thing. And he was ready to attack the guy that was helping them steer their boat. And Jesse calmed him down and it was learned later that the rudder, the steering pin had broken off and so they were totally at the river's mercy and got caught in that whirlpool and sucked in. So, it was not planned. They didn't know, this is a cultural thing, this has to do with understanding the signs of your place. They didn't read the*

traffic signs along the river. On the cliffs were the sign of the river devil that the Indians had carved as petroglyphs on the rocks. Whenever you saw that, that literally means 'what belongs to the river belongs to the river.' Don't try to save someone because if they have gone into the drink the river has claimed them already so you let that be. The water devil is what belongs to the river. The river can just claim you if it wants to. So, if they had known what that meant, they would have known that there were whirlpools in there. It was very treacherous. The Indians may have been using Chinook jargon to extend and communicate with them using that common language to explain that it was a dangerous place and it was pretty clear to see that it was dangerous. Jesse was good with dealing with language and yet he was suspicious of this incident and only later found that they were innocent. Those kinds of things, misreading what previous cultures have shown you and what was done to describe the wilderness, was not understood by the settler."

By all accounts, with the second wave of grief came acceptance. Both Charles and Jesse had lost children before they had even left Missouri; it was a not-uncommon tragedy even in the best of times. Winter was pressing south, sending a steady channel of cold, relentless wind through the river's gorge. They would have to press on through their mourning to reach the relative safety of the Willamette Valley before winter. They turned their backs to the insistent wind and moved on down the river. West.

Four weeks later they arrived at Fort Vancouver, near the confluence of the Willamette and Columbia rivers. They had seen the elephant, but they had made it. They had made it, but their hearts were broken. They were determined that as soon as their families were settled, they would look for another, safer path for future emigrants to travel.

FIVE

"WESTWARD I GO FREE," 1840–1849

Hunting the beaver to extinction and telling wild tales about "savage Indians" could only keep people away for so long, and the English Empire knew that. In the second quarter of the 1800s, the population of the United States was exploding. As more and more people arrived on its eastern shores, more and more pushed west, first into the Appalachian Mountains and then out onto the plains, looking for elbow room and Jefferson's promise of untrammeled liberty.

For the United States, being suddenly land rich had changed everything, even if that land was, as Congressman Daniel Webster described it, "a region of savages and wild beasts, of deserts of shifting sands and whirlpools of dust, of cactus and prairie dogs." There was now seemingly no end of places to claim for oneself. To the English Empire, it appeared the United States was inflating like a massive balloon. A new state was being ratified nearly every two and half years, and it was only a matter of time before they began to encroach on the Empire's fragile hold on Oregon Territory. Once candidate James Polk staked his 1844 presidential campaign on the issue of expansion, running on the slogan "54-40 or Fight," a reference to the northernmost latitude of Oregon Country at the time, and won, it became clear that the

United States was willing to go to war over its Manifest Destiny. Though he declared in his inaugural address that it was his duty "to assert and maintain...the rights of the United States to that portion of our territory which lies beyond the Rocky Mountains," Polk knew that waging such a war in a place hardly anyone had heard of, much less seen, would be expensive and ultimately unpopular.

Instead, he decided to gain possession and control by sheer force of numbers. He put out a call to the mostly newly arrived American people to venture forth and boldly claim what he asserted was rightfully theirs, the whole of the continent south of at least the 49th parallel, the approximate line of the current southern border of Canada. In order to achieve this Manifest Destiny, he told them, the United States needed to "Occupy Oregon."

It may have been intoxicating enough rhetoric to move people at the polls, but few people wanted to venture so far, give up so much, or fight so hard for survival. In the established east, people lived in the comfort of the new industrial age, with indoor plumbing, gas lighting, and heated houses. In their newly constructed cities, there were sidewalks and plazas and opera houses and cathedrals, theaters and high art and music and dance. Theirs was a society of newness and innovation that was taking full advantage of the fruits of all that scientific thinking of the previous decades, gladly embracing technology in the telegraph, typewriters, and cameras. Why would one want to travel thousands of miles and several hundred years into the past when modernity was being invented in front of your very eyes in this burgeoning new country? And once you arrived, what then? You were cast so far afield from your home, your family, your community, to live like that in seclusion and solitude until the end of your days—for what? It was a venture for the desperate or the mad, surely.

Luckily for Polk, there was another movement besides industrialization, one that stood in stark contrast to it, that was sweeping the country: religious fanaticism. As quickly as new scientific discoveries were being made, new, predominantly Christian, religions were being formed, and participation in religious thought and practice in general was on the rise. Important among them were the Methodists and Mormons, Seventh Day Adventists, New Thought, Unitarian Universalism, Reformed Mennonites, and various branches of the Amish as well as the Shakers. Why? Why not? The American people had been inventing and reinventing themselves and redefining what a society could and should look like since the Declaration of Independence. These new religions reflected a national desire for a unique, American way of living rooted in purely American values and traditions, one that would lead them to the promised land, wherever that may be.

That their booming sense of religious purpose coincided with the United States' sudden and urgent need for housing and land for its rapidly growing population was convenient for the federal government and for large corporations with their eyes on the west's natural resources. They realized they could use these people of faith and determination to occupy and hold the land. So, they created programs that allowed and encouraged that to happen.

It required a massive reorganization of the status quo. First, in 1828 Congress designated the land that would become Oklahoma as Indian Territory, forcing out previously established white settlers. Then, the 1830 Indian Removal Act relocated all Indigenous people east of the Mississippi River west to make room for railroads, commercial farming, and cotton plantations, all fueled by the free labor of enslaved people. The vast majority of the Indigenous tribes, Cherokee, Choctaw, Creek, Seminole, among many others, fought the displacement, but it was like fighting the tide. Finally, in 1850 the Oregon Donation Land Act was enacted with the goal of promoting homesteading. It granted free land to "Whites and half-breed Indians" in the Oregon Territory. The message was clear: Go west, all of you.

The government paired those policies with a robust rhetoric of Manifest Destiny, which fed renewed direction (west) and purpose into the old colonial vision of taming and claiming the promised land. Eventually, the promise of religious freedom and tales of nearly naked, presumably godless, roaming people in the far west drew the land-pilgrim's attention. In the west, missionaries like the Whitmans imagined, they could live in peace while satisfying their social doctrines of outreach, piety, and righteousness by imposing their religious ideals and still very European ways of life on the region's Indigenous peoples. Surely, the missionaries thought, these people would welcome the grace of God and the chance to be saved from their savagery. In this way, the first true wave of American people to go west did so with a perspective of the land that stood in direct contrast to the scientific paradigm of the previous half century. Contrary to the scientific expeditions that came before them, missionaries ventured forth not in appreciation of its botanical diversity or in search of geologic wonders, but because of old systems of beliefs in new packages.

What was it they expected to find to the west?

Eden in an unused land. On this point, the early far-west pioneers used the same magical thinking as the original colonists, needing only to see wildness, not emptiness, to assign disuse. Like the early colonists, the actual experience of emigration and life out west was harsh. But the challenges proved to be galvanizing. They remained just as convinced in their moral certainty upon homesteading as they had been when they set out, and just as determined to draw the eastern population out with them.

There were more similarities. They had traveled west in much the same way the earliest European explorers had before them—with maps, fantastical and incomplete. Early emigrant maps of the west were as much about belief and stories than anything else in that time. Those maps had been drawn and redrawn so many times over the first half of the century as colonial powers fought over and bargained with the land, that most of what was depicted, like the old mappae mundi, was still largely the stuff of hearsay and mountain-man legend. But it was also still largely described as the promised land.

The promised land. Heaven. Eden. Not some wild, ungodly place filled with nothing but terror and the hardships of survival, but a land of opportunity and independence. These were the maps into which the emigrants on those first midcentury wagon trains boldly and blindly stepped. These maps drew out more than religious zealots. Some were simply secular refugees searching for escape from what they saw as the physical and spiritual degradation of humanity to the east, ordinary people in search of utopia.

By the 1840s, the question of just what kind of nation the country could, or should, or might become was still a matter of debate, particularly as a large swath of the country clung to the morally bankrupt practice of slavery. It was a time of rapid change, of fevers, fanatics, zealots, reformers, and eccentrics. People were hungry for new ways of thinking and being and for the radical acceptance of the self, and this was expressed in a multitude of new ways of living. Vegetarianism and teetotaling were common, just as were circuses and freak shows. In comparison to the scientific thinkers of the previous half century, the midcentury American public was a mystical and otherworldly focused people that saw the enlightenment as the harbinger of a dystopian industrial age. They railed against the crowding and dismal conditions of the eastern cities whose cholera outbreaks were prompting quarantines and whose air was thick with pollution. They lamented that the early pristine abundance of the eastern lands had faded and been replaced with slums and cesspools. They were right. Many, many people lived in smoggy, overcrowded squalor without access to clean water and little hope of upward mobility.

The idea of establishing a new life of their own design out west, the tale spun for them by the missionaries, had by then begun to sit well with many of these forward thinkers. Some of them took action and followed the missionaries and their maps out through the plains, into the deserts, and over the mountains in search of arable land, a self-sufficient lifestyle, and a wild and ecstatic kind of grace. It was a far from utopian experience. Instead, it was a costly and horrific journey followed by an even harder life in nowhere near unoccupied country that they would soon have to take up arms to hold. But not yet. The arrival of the missionaries had been brutal enough in the beginning, as the native populations were initially decimated by emigrant disease. But that stark reality would not be the story imprinted on the new American cultural identity.

Instead, to the east, a different narrative of the wilderness, and by proxy the west, was being crafted by a group of thinkers, activists, and artists that would change the way the American public related to and defined wilderness for the next 150 years. Enter Walt Whitman, Ralph Waldo Emerson, Henry David Thoreau, Edgar Allan Poe, and other poets and painters, visual influencers of the day from the Hudson School of painting, like Frederic Church. These mostly white men spent their time in and around New England, especially Concord, Massachusetts, and were each other's instructors, mentors, companions, and conspirators. They were activists, promoting radical personal freedoms, race and gender equality, and freedom from government—they were vehemently antitax and antislavery. They lectured and toured and promoted themselves and one another, and they did so from what was arguably the center of academic thought in America at that time and well into the twentieth century. Together, they were the Transcendentalists.

Transcendentalism originated out of the Unitarian Universalist movement. Relying on Eastern philosophy and religions, it held that a spiritual state, characterized by ecstasy, vivid experience, and passion was the path to enlightenment. More specifically, Transcendentalists believed, like the mid-century emigrants, that this kind of ecstatic grace could be found in nature, that in experiencing the natural world, one participated in a kind of secular liturgy in the common man's cathedral. Also like the emigrants west, they believed in self-reliance and harbored a healthy distrust of government and industrialization. But what set them apart was their belief in and embrace of science, scientific inquiry, and the study of natural systems as an extension of and natural partner to their spirituality. In particular, they were influenced by Humboldt's Kosmos theory (only newly translated into English several decades after its first publication) that everything in the universe is connected and essential to a system that is fundamentally greater than the sum of its parts. That embracing of both the scientific and spiritual zeitgeists of the time made transcendentalism as a theory wildly palatable and popular. Like the emigrants and other zealots of the time, however, putting the tenets of transcendentalism into practice would prove as complicated as emigration west.

Many of the Transcendentalists spent time in communes, living closely to the land. In 1843, the same year the Applegates and hundreds of others followed Marcus Whitman to Oregon in the Great Migration and just a year before the murder of Joseph Smith would spur the Mormons to strike out for the Great Salt Lake, a group of transcendentalists that included Emerson purchased a ninety-acre farm they called Fruitlands in Harvard, Massachusetts. There, they lived communally and intentionally, with the goal of achieving self-sustainability and adopting a way of life based on utopian values and ethics that mirrored those of the western missionaries and religious zealots of the time. But like the early colonists and the settlers after them, the experiment disintegrated quickly, and for much the same reasons. "Their whole doctrine is spiritual," Emerson would later write of Fruitlands, "but they always end with saying, give us much land and money." The west, in contrast, did not offer the luxury of falling apart, which, be it on the road or once settled, was a lethal option, not just part of a utopian experiment.

The most famous of these transcendental retreats to the land was Thoreau's. Thoreau, himself a surveyor like Humboldt and the Applegates, is famous for spending a year of solitude in the woods by Walden Pond, surviving, presumably, through his own labor and in isolation. But it was a bit of a farce. He was not in the wilds of the American landscape; he was in a haggard wood nestled between a lake and a pastoral, fenced landscape on the outskirts of Concord. There, he built a rudimentary cabin where he wrote, chopped wood, and walked along the lakeside. What came of that time, *Walden*, was a treatise on solitude, simplicity, nature, and the passage of time as marked by the seasons. But Thoreau also entertained visitors and threw parties. And his sister and mother performed the majority of his laundry and housework chores, often bringing him his meals as well. That the land was Emerson's, and that Thoreau characterized himself as a "squatter" on the land was no matter, nor was his privileged perspective.

This is not to say that his perspective was invalid, or even that he was not willing to sacrifice or place himself at risk for his ideals. Thoreau was jailed for his refusal to pay taxes, and he was a conductor on the Underground Railroad. He was not complicit in the farce. He often spoke and wrote about his preference for the pastoral, cultivated woods over that of the raw wilderness he experienced in other locations. Those places, he admitted, filled him not with the ecstatic grace for which he searched, but fear. Regardless of his own experiences however, he never stopped proclaiming the virtues of the pristine wilderness, untouched and unexperienced by man except in his mind's eye, and he never stopped exalting the myth of the "logger's path and the Indian trail."

The public ate it up as a call to the wild, when in fact it was a call to something altogether more controlled and distant from any real kind of wilderness. Many of his contemporaries, the painters and poets, fell to the same poison pill, depicting nature as a masculinized place of beauty and peace even as the emigrants west abandoned their wagons and lost their children in river fords. It helped create a mythology of the American wilderness that permeated the changing American consciousness and encouraged the average person to abandon the notion of survival in the wild and instead seek these places out for leisure and renewal.

The effect it had on the general public was to deconstruct the paradigm of the wild as a dangerous and untamed place and instead reinvent it as a place of celebration, freedom, and spiritual levity, especially in the west, of which Thoreau said: "Eastward I go only by force, but westward I go free. This is the prevailing tendency of my countrymen. I must walk toward Oregon." And so the people did.

SIGNPOST

While east-coast cities of the mid-eighteenth century grew into sophisticated urban centers, the west remained not only largely unpopulated by American citizens but contested by foreign powers and Indigenous people. As the industrial revolution increased access to these western lands, it became increasingly important for the United States to establish ownership and control. The single northern route to Oregon country would not be enough to hold the region; a southern route had to be established.

SIX

TRAIL STORY: GOD, GOLD, AND THAT DAMNABLE APPLEGATE ROAD

THE END OF THE OREGON TRAIL, AS EXPERIENCED BY THE Applegates, was the rocky basalt plateau of a point bar overlooking the Willamette River south of its confluence with the Columbia in the middle of some 50,000 square miles of unmapped country. There, dense stands of Douglas firs mixed with other conifers, giant western red cedars whose bark pulled off in thin strips, hemlock, and pines. Around them on all sides were rivers, fed by constant rain and snowmelt that poured off the high peaks in the distance. Behind them sat the volcanoes of the Cascade Range. To the west, high rumpled ridges of the coast range, uplifted seafloor composed of limestones, sandstones, and shales rich with fossils. Often, low, impenetrable cloud cover obscured these features from view for days and even weeks at a time.

For weary travelers like the Applegates looking for a place to settle, there was only one direction to go—south, down the wide, flat-bottomed valley that sutured the two ranges together. The valley floor is composed of flood deposits, silts and clays from the Willamette River. It is rich, fertile ground that, once cleared, promised abundant crops for anyone willing to work the land and shoulder through the region's nine-month rainy season.

They cast their mind's eyes into the valley and envisioned the future.

In that future were summer fields golden brown with wheat standing in sharp definition on the shaft or fiery-red with crimson clover interlaced with long lines of hops, orchards bursting with hazelnuts and apples, and fields of pumpkins and corn in fall. Overhead, bald eagles circling, their babies screaming for food from nearby nests as coyote leaped beneath them in high, diving arcs after their prey. On what few rises exist across the landscape, houses, whitewashed and meticulously kept, a row of rose bushes dotting the end of every property, weeping willows forming natural gazebos in every yard. Beyond the houses, the faintest outline of a town. Someday.

The immediate problem, though, was survival. So the group pushed on, eventually taking up winter residence near the old abandoned Methodist Mission. From there, they could search for homesteads. The mission, a collection of squat log buildings in close formation, left much to be desired after so long a journey. Methodists had built it in 1834. They were pilgrims looking for a simpler life and a place to proselytize without interference. It hadn't worked out the way they hoped and eventually the missionaries had moved on. Now the mission served as shelter for whomever came upon them and a gathering place for nearby homesteaders. The plain wooden buildings did little to keep out Oregon's cold rains, but it would have to do.

When the Applegates arrived, it was also the site of a burgeoning government and economy organized by the Americans residing in Oregon Country. In those earliest years, most everyone was either a missionary or a trapper, and in many respects the Applegates and their companions in that first wagon train were not so different. They were moral people of some faith who had traveled well in the company of missionaries like Marcus Whitman. Now safely in the valley, the brothers got to work. Charles, his wife, Melinda, already pregnant with another child, worked as a blacksmith that first winter. Jesse worked as surveyor general for the territory and, as his friend Robert Shortess had predicted in his letters enticing him to make the journey, was easily elected to the legislative assembly. Lindsay had operated a grist mill in St. Louis and figured he'd do the same in Oregon, but he wasn't opposed to going wherever the wind blew him. All three kept their eyes out for their ideal homestead.

Meanwhile, each year more and more new immigrants poured into Oregon territory, many recounting similar stories of misery and dangerous conditions on the overland trail and death and disasters on the river. In one incident, an entire family of travelers drowned trying to navigate the same river run that had taken the Applegate's children. The brothers continued to insist there had to be a better passage.

As the population grew, the provisional government worked towards statehood. Complicating the matter was the issue of boundaries. At the time, Oregon was still disputed territory, especially towards the south where few American had taken up homesteads. To hold the territory and define its borders, the United States would likely have to take up arms against either Spain or Great Britain. But there was no land access to the disputed borderlands and no way to transport goods or military men and munitions without taking the cumbersome northern route or relying on ships. They needed a southern road.

The Applegates loved the idea. They saw the government's

plans for a southern road as an opportunity to establish the new, safer route that avoided the Columbia River they had hoped for. It seemed likely that such a route existed. Mountain men, hunters, and trappers had been using a network of Indigenous people's foot trails throughout the region for decades. Charting a southern road might only be a matter of connecting the trails. Some of the trail network had even been mapped. Surely such a route east could be found. Jesse seized on the idea and introduced legislation that would fund a road hunting expedition. The legislation passed, but Oregon Country would refuse to yield.

South of the mission, the Willamette Valley begins to gradually narrow as the opposing peaks and ridgelines of the Cascades and the Coast Range close together, and the base level of the valley rises up to meet the river's headwaters. Eventually, the valley disappears altogether and the landscape becomes a crumpled mess of deeply incised rock layers. Southern Oregon is a geologic meeting place, where the massive granite plutons of the Sierra Nevada's merge with the explosive peaks of the Cascades, and uplifted stacks of ancient sea floor are heaped over and against one another. At high altitudes, which is most places there, the close proximity of the ocean brings heavy and persistent winter snows. The window for travel in such country is short, and sudden snowstorms are common and deadly.

This was a lesson the emigrants learned the hard way. The first year, the Territorial government sent a group who got as far as the Siskiyous but were pushed back by deep snow. "Whilst on the one hand we learn with regret that the company of road hunters which started from Polk County, has returned unsuccessful and discouraged; on the other, we are cheered with the intelligence, that another party…is forming, and will soon be prepared to start, under the command of an able and experienced pilot," the *Spectator* announced on June 25, 1846. That able and experienced pilot was Jesse Applegate.

Undeterred, Jesse and Lindsay, and a company of just over a dozen men set out along those old trails with Jesse as the surveyor and Lindsay along with him as a scout (they had left Charles at home with the three families). The brothers brought with them a Hudson's Bay Company trapper route map from 1827—their modern maps simply labeled the area they were to navigate as an "unexplored region." Jesse, as navigator and the provisional government's representative, led the group. He knew that his capacity as an elected official would put him under scrutiny. In those days everything, from government business to gossip, was published in the papers. Before their departure they had published high praise for the expedition, the brothers, and Jesse in particular, naming him 'first citizen of Oregon' and touting his expertise as a 'road hunter.' His survey skills, everyone hoped, would be the key to the group's success. But Jesse knew that if they, like the earlier group that had attempted to find the route, failed, it would also be put on him. It was his name on the legislation.

The group did well at first, making the relatively easy climb out of the Willamette valley and following somewhat mapped trails into the Umpqua Mountains. But there, they began to doubt if a true road, one suitable for large groups of soldiers and their equipment or wagons and families was possible. The canyons were narrow and the ground surface was littered with loose rock, boulders, and fallen trees. It was hard going in good weather by strong men on foot. But they knew that the other side of the mountains were less rugged, that the weather was better, and that it opened onto the flatlands of the high desert. They remained sure that a navigable route through the mountains existed. They just had to find it.

They were right. A passable route did exist, mostly. Almost certainly with some improvements, which they were sure could be completed quickly. It wouldn't be a pretty road, but it would be a serviceable one. Even with its rough edges the brothers were sure it would be safer than the northern river route. By fall they reached the head of the California Trail near the Humboldt River, proving to themselves, at least, that passage was possible. There, the company split ways. One group was to prepare the trail for wagons, the other was to carry on east to Fort Hall, Idaho, to promote the new route and act as guides. But failure of communication, prior obligations, and lack of dedication got the better of them. Some men, including, perhaps, the Applegates, broke from the group early to return home to care for livestock, attend to business matters, or act as hired hands to weary emigrants. Historical records regarding the events are incomplete and contradictory. The subsequent effects though, are excruciatingly clear.

Members of the forward company, including Jesse, made it to Fort Hall, and began to recruit travelers to try their new route and sell them additional supplies. All told, at least a hundred wagons, around two hundred people, followed their advice and turned onto the new trail. Setting out with Levi Scott, a member of the road hunter team as a guide, they had no idea that somehow, some portions of the trail hadn't been improved. They would have to clear portions of the largely unmarked path themselves. In his journal and later letters Scott recounts being surprised by the lack of improvements and the struggle he and the other men in the train faced each day to clear the road and get the group over the mountains before winter. It made for incredibly slow going and along with that, everything else that could go wrong would.

First, the Indigenous people through whose lands the road cut launched a justified campaign of harassment in protest of this encroachment on their territory. Next, the sparse vegetation of the rocky terrain proved too thin to graze the cattle. Then, abnormally heavy spring rains and record snowfall blanketed the region. Creeks that had been dry when the road hunters first passed now surged with water and the ground turned to slick mud, miring oxen, wagons, and people. Then bitter cold and high winds descended mounting the snow into massive, impassable drifts. Supplies and energy ran low. Livestock froze; wagons had to be abandoned. Finally, the train stopped making any progress at all. They were stranded.

But some people, trappers and scouts more familiar with the terrain and unencumbered by children, livestock, and possessions, made their way into the populated valley. When they informed the people there of the disaster unfolding in the mountains several rescue attempts were made, one even led by the Applegates. In the end, many completed the journey, though some on foot with only the few possessions they could carry. Others didn't survive.

Those who survived turned on the road hunters, the Applegates most of all, accusing them of being grifters and road pirates in newspapers and pamphlets. Some even insisted that the men had known all along the company would be stranded and had lured them onto the road anyway. One member of the train was especially vocal. Jesse Quinn Thornton, a wealthy lawyer and acknowledged "peevish grump" who had lost all his belongings (including, as he itemized, a medicine chest, cut-glass bottles, and a cast-steel spade), grabbed onto the issue and wouldn't let go. He focused his rage on the Applegates, whom he claimed, somewhat rightly, were the responsible parties. For months he published piece after piece in the papers, decrying Jesse Applegate, his team, and "that damnable Applegate Road."

That the road was considered a failure, that lives had been lost, and that they were considered to blame pained the Applegates and only compounded their suffering from losing their own boys to the northern route. Their intentions had been motivated by grief, a heartfelt conviction that no other family should lose a loved one on the way to Oregon. They were distressed that their path had caused such suffering and loss of human life. That anyone would suspect them of ill intent, of grifting, was devastating. Their allies were many though, and the many members of the party stuck together, defending the condition of the trail at the start of the season and pointing to the late nature of the final train's arrival to the mountains, the early storm that caused them to get stuck, and the particularly harsh winter that had made rescue difficult.

It sparked a public debate that very nearly ended in bloodshed when, James W. Nesmith, who had arrived in Oregon Country with the Applegates in 1843, enraged at the continued assassination of the Applegates' character that he challenged Thornton to a duel. Thornton, a man of many words but apparently little action, ignored the challenge. But Nesmith persisted peppering settlements and farms throughout Oregon Territory with handbills denouncing Thornton:

TO THE WORLD!!

J. Quinn Thornton,

Having resorted to low, cowardly and dishonorable means, for the purpose of injuring my character and standing, and having refused honorable satisfaction, which I have demanded; I avail myself of this opportunity of publishing him to the world as a reclaimless liar, an infamous scoundrel, a black hearted villain, an arrant coward, a worthless vagabond and an imported miscreant, a disgrace to the profession and a dishonor to his country.

James W. Nesmith, Oregon City, June 7, 1847

The duel never happened. A ban on dueling between office-holders, which both men were, had been passed by the provisional government in 1845 when, according to the Legislative Policy and Research Office, "committee member Jessie Applegate presented a bill to prohibit dueling, and within half an hour the measure was signed by the Governor." The Applegates had preemptively saved Thornton, Nesmith, and to some degree, themselves.

Thornton was bitter and cantankerous sure, and he *had* suffered along the trail, just not necessarily because of the Applegates. They were simply bearing the brunt of his anger. In truth, he might have counted himself lucky. The same storm that had caught him up had also caught the party from which he and his wife had split from following a fight he had had with his then business partner. The whole thing had been a mess from the beginning.

That company, filled with wealthy families and businessmen, left late, more than a month after the usual departure date. At Fort Hall, the men of the group were approached by a man claiming to have found a shorter way through the mountains, a new route which he insisted was a shortcut. They were aware of the perils of trying to navigate the western mountains late in the season. So, they detoured, heading south. But the trail proved hard to find and even harder to navigate. They stalled and backtracked, losing another month and gaining little by way of forward progress. It wasn't a situation conducive to friendly relations and the individual groups that made up the party were beginning to squabble. And they had lost some cattle in a raid, which only served to fray nerves further. By the time they reached the Humboldt Sink they were dangerously late and running low on provisions. Thornton was not the only one complaining, but by all accounts, he was the loudest, so when the Applegate Road party showed up talking about a new road of their own, he was quick to join them, even if they were going to Oregon instead of California.

The rest of the company continued on without Thornton. It was early November, too late, most previous emigrants would have told them. But they had come so far already, surely their luck would change. All they had to do was make it over the mountains before the winter snows set in. It was a losing gamble. Their luck did not change. Instead, they continued to See the Elephant, facing illness, attack, and injury as they struggled to find their way. Some of the families had to abandon their wagons, leaving behind potentially lifesaving supplies and shelter. By all accounts, the animosity between the parties had only grown with time, and help was not readily forthcoming nor free among them. Businessmen, after all, will be businessmen. It's said that better-faring parties kept close tabs on loans made to fellow travelers. They made dismal progress, sometimes less than a mile a day.

Just as the party—about eighty-five people, mostly from the Donner and Reed families—made it to the crest of the Sierra Nevada mountains, a winter storm hit. Differences in pacing had already divided the party in two, so when they became mired in snow and were forced to stop, they were in two groups nearly a mile apart from one another. The weather got worse and the snow got deeper and the winds blew and it became clear that no one was going anywhere. So they made camp, or what would have to pass for a camp, stretching animal hides over hastily constructed wooden frames. Surely it would get them through the storm. But four weeks later, they were still there.

The situation was clearly untenable and the winter weather was seemingly endless. It was decided that some of them, at least, would have to try and make it out. The healthiest or bravest or most desperate of the men determined to go and set about fashioning simple snowshoes from branches. It was a good idea and seemed to work, but again luck wasn't with them. What little visibility they had was erased by snow blindness and the previous weeks had drained them of vitality. Most of the men that set out died. Back at the pass the group, now mostly children, was starving. Their food had been gone for days and the snows prevented any hunting or scavenging, which they didn't have the strength for anyway. They ate bark and handfuls of snow to fill their bellies. Then they ate the leather from their clothing. Weeks later, desperation would drive them to eat the covers of their shelters.

Somehow, word of a wagon company trapped in the mountains made its way to the valley but it took until February for the first rescue attempt to be made. When they arrived, it was clear that most of the group was too weak to make the trip out, so they were left with provisions and a promise that the rescuers would come back for them. Once again on their own, their bad luck returned. Animals, suffering through the same brutal winter conditions, found and devoured the food the rescuers had left. That's when the party took to eating the snow-preserved flesh from their fellow travelers' lifeless bodies. They were careful that no one ate a relative. One man, filled with hunger and the dehumanizing racism of colonial wilderness, shot and ate the two Indigenous men who had accompanied them.

By spring, only forty-eight members of the party, nearly all children, survived.

To the north, there was another kind of trouble. Measles had broken out at the Whitman mission, killing far more Indigenous people than white people. The loss inflamed the already tense relations between the two groups. In retaliation, a group of Cayuse attacked the mission, taking the women and children hostage and killing more than a dozen men, including Marcus Whitman. The press picked up the story, calling it a massacre, and the pioneer population took violent action in response, publicly hanging five Cayuse men. With that, the Cayuse declared war. It became clear that the great missionary experiment was as much a failure as the new Applegate Road.

Soon though, came redemption, at least for the trail. In 1848 more than half the men of Oregon and thousands of others arriving from parts east would come to use at least some portion of the trail, and without complaint. At long last, the promises of Christopher Columbus had come true. There was gold in California.

It was a frenzy. As soon as word of gold in California arrived, a primal hunger kicked in. Men began loading wagons, this time without their women and children. In Oregon, the new Applegate Road no longer served as a lengthy bypass, but rather as a connector to the already established trapper routes from southern Oregon straight into the heart of gold country. There was no need to take the portion of the trail over the eastern pass that had caused so much trouble. Likewise, those arriving from the east now turned off the Applegate Trail just miles from its origin at any number of cutoff roads in the Nevada desert toward the gold fields. The "great divergence" it was called.

And just like that, the Applegate Trail faded from history.

SEVEN

FEEDING THE B(EAST), 1850–1891

WAGON ROADS WERE FOR SUCKERS. THE DONNER PARTY HAD made that clear. Ultimately, though, none of it really mattered. The end of the rainbow had finally been found, and it was in California. When people heard the news of gold in its hills, all the invention and fever and radical reform of the previous half century gave way as gold thirst replaced the wild-eyed, corpse-eating hunger of the emigrants. And you could forget about going west in search of redemption, Eden, grace, or even simplicity. Those were lofty ideals, sure, lovely and compelling myths that eastern urbanites and mid-country settlers could cling to when dreaming of escape from the drudgery of daily life. But true wilderness, the kind they had been told could only be found in the west, had proven that it truly was not a place for families. It was a place for men, able bodied and ambitious, a place where fortunes were found, not God. No, it would be for the love of gold, not God, that the whole world would go west, and they would do so regardless of the risks, even if they had to book passage around South America to get there.

With so many people rushing to stake their claim, you didn't even have to be a miner to strike it rich. Real entrepreneurs knew you could make your fortune pushing pickaxes, liquor, or 'ladies of the line'…and it would be a heck of a lot easier and a whole lot more fun.

For the first time, Americans cast their gaze not across the surface of the west, but into it, desperate to divine the subsurface location of mineral and ore deposits, water, metals, and gold—black or yellow. Cross sections and topography, not townships and ranges, were what they needed; there was economic power in three-dimensionality. It's not an exact science. Cross sections are where imagination, geometry, and geosciences come together to predict the below-surface features of the landscape, as transected by a vertical plane. To an experienced eye, what may seem at the surface to be linear stripes of varying rock types is actually the bedded rock layers of a U-shaped fold under the ground. Why might anyone care about such folds? The apices of those folds are geologic collection zones, where fluids like oil and water can accumulate. Those fluids have traveled long distances underground to these folds, picking up dissolved minerals and metals as they go. When they reach a fold apex, they stop moving, often changing temperatures when they do. Those conditional changes cause the precipitation of the dissolved elements. Which means, often, there's gold in those folds. Cross sections answer hungry questions like where, how much, and how hard will it be to get to, and in the latter half of the nineteenth century, Americans were hungry.

So, like the Donner Party, the United States in the second half of the 1800s began to eat itself.

First to the table were the corporations. Corporations had, for the previous half century, been perhaps the only things in the United States growing faster than the population, a phenomenon that accelerated in the midcentury. The government knew that the labor, infrastructure, and capital required to extract resources on the kind of industrial scale needed to satisfy the rapidly growing cities to the east could only be found in corporations. For the corporations, it was political leverage and they used it to their advantage. It created its own kind of gold rush, with more corporations than ever before forming in response to eased restrictions on who could launch such an endeavor. Premier among these new corporations were pushers of infrastructure in eastern cities, westward-bound railroads, manufacturers, and utility companies. The practices employed by these companies were often questionable, but the profits were astronomical.

There was a problem, at least for the corporations. Private land ownership, as opposed to mere settlement and occupation, had become mandatory, and land-control practices had evolved; mining claims, water rights, and homesteading were all strictly regulated. Between the calls to occupy Oregon and the discovery of gold, much of the land had already been claimed by individuals. The rigidly mapped rectangles of township and range now extended across the entirety of the map. But there were ways around that, especially if you had the federal government under your thumb, which they did.

It was true that the Homestead Act of 1862 had allowed any adult who had never taken up arms against the federal government to claim land, provided they occupied, cultivated, and improved it for a period of five years. And it *had* resulted in a massive transfer of land into private hands. In fact, nearly one-tenth of the total land area of the United States was, by midcentury, held in legal (almost entirely white and male) ownership. But homesteading was harder than most thought it would be. Many of these ventures quickly fell apart, as homesteaders failed to make the required payments, died, returned home, or abandoned their land to join the gold rush. Of those who stayed on, many small farms struggled to keep pace with the mechanization of agricultural practices, and with so much arable land available, agricultural prices were beginning to drop. It was easy to fail. Knowing that, the corporations, especially the railroads, increasingly pressed for legislation and policy that protected their rights and increased their control over land use. Eminent domain, the concept of individual land rights being usurped by government and, as an extension, corporations, became normative practice. With the massive influx of people to California, corporations saw their chance to take not just control over, but actual ownership of, the west. Besides, the powers that be back east were financially overextended and distracted with the tasks of abolition and, hopefully, reconstruction. If they moved fast, they could steal the land even before the stealing was done. And that's just what they did, conspiring and colluding with one another to consolidate and control their industries.

It wasn't just California. When gold was discovered along a portion of the Applegate Trail, a lot of people were given a lot of grubstake to make the hard trip up to Oregon and work the ground. *Grubstake*. Shorthand for where your food and backing were coming from, and who was entitled to a piece of your profits. If you had any profits. Which most didn't. There was never a map you could rely on, never a clear view into the earth to see what was below, and there was a lot of big talk, fast talk, and downright lies— not a lot of real information. They were all groping in the dark like those miserable emigrants trying to get over the passes with no way to know if you were being thrown off the track of a good claim or being dealt a square deal.

The grubstake prospectors were pretty much as uniformly terrible miners as they were uniformly male. They were soft, to start, hungry and wild eyed from the journey, and completely lacking in any applicable experience or know-how. Most relied on what they could glean from how-to manuals or from watching other miners, in particular the wave of Chinese emigrants arriving as fast or faster over water as European emigrants were over land. They, more often than not, did know what they were doing.

It didn't have to be an elaborate process; gold sinks fast and shines bright, so water and gravity could do most of the work, you just had to know how to use it to your advantage. At some sites you could just wade in the water with a pan, swirling the already sorted sediments until the gold came together and could be picked out. But panning was for small dreamers, men that couldn't get a grubstake, or those that had been taken. Volume was the key. Managing water, the need for it, or its disposal, was the hardest part, requiring digging ditches and fashioning sluice boxes to channel water and sort the sediment. That and finding a place to pile the tailings. Mind you, you had to stake your claim first. And protect it. Claim jumping was the rule, not the exception. Those who did hit a lode worked the land to exhaustion. The tailing piles grew into massive structures, and wing dams were constructed to divert entire streams and portions of larger rivers into shallow, slow-moving ponds, piles of logs and boulders shifting the natural relationship of water and gravity across the land. Overhead and alongside chain pumps, lines of buckets on pulleys powered by wooden paddle wheels, bailed water from the pools, preventing them from overtopping and returning the water to its stream.

Where water was in abundance, the men used high-powered nozzles to scour the rock from slopes. In other places, where water was scarce, ditches were dug for yards or even miles, terminating in shallow hand-dug pools that retained the water above the dry diggings. When the reservoir was full, the men would wait at the base of the slope with shovels and trowels and rakes and sorters until the reservoir was broken open and the water rushed out in a single torrent. At night, the work continued illuminated by bonfires.

When the homesteaders and easy diggings were gone, the men packed up their wagons and moved on. The land rested. That's when the corporations moved in, ready to buy up the spent land, and in doing so, providing much-needed capital to all those farmers—and trail-weary gold diggers—all by then just as much dejected failures as were the early wagon pioneers. It seemed for a time that nature had won. But not for long. Trains were coming, and fast, bringing with them those families who hadn't materialized in the frenzied burning of all that grubstake. The railroad companies were sure that if transcontinental lines went in, a new wave of prospectors, the wives and children of those that remained, and everything else, would follow. But they would need a gradable route, and for that, they had their eyes on the southern emigrant routes, the Applegate and California trails. In the battle between man and nature, they were sure that nature would, in time, be overwhelmed.

First came the reconnaissance parties, surveyors, scientists, and artists. They passed through like a whisper, hardly noticed by man or beast as they followed the ruts, sighting and measuring, pacing out, sampling, collecting, painting, documenting everything and anything in a great accounting. Finally, they passed, and for what seemed like an eternity, nothing much changed. The remaining grubstakers grubbed at the land, the claim jumpers jumped claims, and the wagons rolled, though these had slowed from a gushing tide to a wearied trickle. The ruts sank into the soil. Sluice water snaked down drainages.

That land, the land area given to homesteaders, amounted to about 50 million acres, and even if the corporations had been able to buy it all, it still wasn't nearly enough. No matter. When the Pacific Railroad Acts passed, the government turned over 100 million acres of land to the railroads at no cost at all. Two years later they amended the acts to also give over any and all resources along the line. The west was under new ownership.

Americans, those who noticed, didn't seem to mind. Their minds were occupied with the aftermath of the Civil War and the reconstruction, unification, renewal, and redefinition that chapter of history necessitated. If those goals could be achieved through the reclaiming and redivision of the west, if the state of the union could be held together by little more than a strand of telegraph wire and a circuitous track of steel, so be it. The west, unlike the ravaged landscape of the postwar east, still had its shine. For the eastern population, everywhere they looked there was destruction and bloodshed, but to the west, they were increasingly told, was triumph, freedom, gold, and more, if only it could be found. The newly minted Geological Survey with Clarence King at its helm did little to dispel the myth of the west as a buffet, establishing early on the connection between mapping and consumption, stating, "The vast plains will produce something better than buffalo, namely beef; there is water for irrigation, and land fit to receive it. All that is needed is to explore and declare the nature of the national domain."

The railroads, eager to take full advantage of their corporate position with a line reaching from sea to shining sea, were especially devoted to this euphoric and expansionist narrative. The first of the Pacific Railroad Acts passed in 1862, the same year as the first of the Homestead Acts. It authorized the transcontinental railroad project and paid mostly two companies (the Central Pacific Railroad Company of California and Union Pacific), by the mile, to construct it, meeting in no place in particular. Predictably, the two companies and their affiliated industries, starting at either end, took advantage of the situation.

So began the great rending.

It came in a cloud of dust, wagons and horses and men and tents and equipment—hundreds of tons of steel, thousands of thick-cut ties, tons of spikes and joiners. There were wheelbarrows, dump carts, shovels, axes, crowbars, foundry tools, switch mechanisms, telegraph line, and blasting powder and nitroglycerine. And to haul it all, wagons. Wagons for the supplies, wagons for the men, their tents and belongings and provisions. Wagons and teams for hauling and loading and dumping and scraping. Wagons for the overseers, the money men, and the crew bosses. And the wagons rolled and the crews scraped and blasted and filled, cutting switchbacks, blowing through mountains, and constructing trestles. The forward teams clawed and dug at the earth, cutting a miles-long circuitous path through whatever was before them, prairie turf, mudflats, or granite. It was a show of force with no one there to watch as they blasted straight through the bellies of millions of years-old mountains, rocks that had been formed over time in the depths of the ocean before being slowly warped and uplifted. Behind the teams came the hand crews that placed the heavy rails and held them to gauge as the spikers leapfrogged past them with levelers, and the fillers came after them, and all alongside the men raised poles and strung a single, continuous, tenuous strand of telegraph wire. It was an unstable process, and one that claimed the lives of countless workers—how many, no one knows, because no one stopped to ask.

Everywhere they went the trees for miles around came down, gobbled up by the line and the telegraph. There were thousands of laborers, the ambitious Chinese along the western line and the potato-starved Irish from the east, and they all needed housing and fuel and heat. Not that the Chinese workers were given room or board. They were on their own. And then there were the Hell on Wheels towns. Even at a pace of a handful of miles a day, there was plenty of time for rough-and-ready settlements to be built ahead of the progress. These were façade towns, whose primary industries were women, gambling, and booze, and whose buildings were thrown together with whatever was at hand and were often dismantled and hauled away only to be reconstructed farther down the line. From inside the phenomenon, you would never know the rest of the country was fighting a bloody civil war. The war would end someday, and when it did, the railroad companies would be ready.

Except when the Civil War did end, the transcontinental railroad was still a dream, meandering through the west. Even with all the lode from the government coffers, the money was nearly gone. To complete the line, the railroads would need a massive influx of cash. To make it a reality would take a touch. So, Thomas Durant, the vice president of the Union Pacific Railroad, a man with a long history of shady financial dealings, staged a frontier "excursion" at the end of the line, which at that time was still barely making its way out of the Dakotas. There, he gathered journalists, politicians, and barons (robber or otherwise) and thrilled them with a 'spectacle of spectacles' that, he insisted, was accessible only by rail: the laboring Irish workmen laying the line, buffalo hunting from the windows of a train car, an intentionally set prairie fire, and mock raids by Pawnee Indians, complete with high-class meals and fireworks.

Durant's version of the frontier was not all for the sake of bravado. There were real problems. Labor for one, either the estimated 10,000 Chinese or the 3,000 to 5,000 Irish, and "Indians" for another. Not enough of the first, and too many of the other from the railroad's perspective. The solutions were swift and brutal, and the frontier show was designed to make the fixes palatable. Othering the Indigenous people would soothe the public's alarm at their treatment. Killing the buffalo, that most essential of resources to those displaced people, would take care of decimating the population. In his frontier show, Durant invented a new kind of wild west, one that revived the missionary view of 'Indians as savages,' that cast wild beasts as mere fish in barrels, and in which technology could overcome any physical obstacle. The good time that was had by all, he hoped, would be enough to persuade the collected dignitaries to help him solve problems of the "regular" business sort, the greasing of wheels and palms needed to keep the supply chain and the lines moving, and the policy makers making policy in the right direction, which in this case, was west. He bet it all that giving them a wild ride in a western wilderness steeped in romanticism would do the trick. It was a new brand of wild in the west that was all about release, the loosening of belts, purse strings, and mores, elbow room, the staking of claims, and the expansion of new ideas. It worked.

When, finally, the two ends met in the middle, on May 10, 1869, they did so at Promontory Summit in Utah, smack between the Great Salt Lake and the emigrant trail divergence at Fort Hall.

The famous heads of the competing rail lines, Leland Stanford and Thomas Durant, had made the journey out for the event, along with, depending on who you asked, anywhere from 300 to 3,000 government officials, businessmen, and laborers who crowded around the line alongside the dignitaries. The working men looked parched and uncomfortable wearing jackets and waistcoats that hung loosely from their labor-thinned frames as they crowded around the line squinting into the sun. Stanford and Durant would share the honor of sinking the final spike, made of gold especially for the event, into the ground. It was the simplest of tasks, but they both swung and missed. When a rail worker finally got it done, the news went out to the world along a newly live telegraph cable.

And then the owners and businessmen and government dignitaries returned home, and when the money ran out, the Hell on Wheels towns packed it in and all these men, all these people, were suddenly, irrevocably, *there* and sure to be coming faster all the time.

It was a problem. The ripping apart of the land and the gouging of its surface, its restraint by steel and wood, and the constant and violent displacement of its Indigenous inhabitants into what was an increasingly crowded west made it clear that Americans, had no intention of sharing. In justified response, Native Americans sabotaged the railroad and the machinery that built it and attacked the remaining Hell on Wheels towns and homesteads.

It wasn't just along the rail line. It wasn't going much better in Oregon. How many people had shown up when gold was found along the Applegate Road was never exactly nailed down, but it was enough to sound alarm bells for the Rogue and Modoc and dozens of other peoples who had lived in the area for centuries. They took up arms and stayed at arms, even as they were corralled and marched across the land. Many were marched right off the edge of the continent into the frigid waters of the Pacific Ocean. West.

It went on this way for decades. Eventually, the wars reached a stalemate in a lowland valley along the Applegate Road encircled by mountains, at the base of a weathered and eroded lava flow that had been worn away into a horseshoe called Table Rock. From there, the Rogue people made a years-long stand, holding back seemingly the whole enormity of the United States federal government asserting what it took to be its birthright—possession and control over the land between the oceans. They lost.

There was another problem.

When the line was finally completed that hot day in May on Promontory Summit, Durant had cemented the relationship between the railroad and the "wild" west in the American mind. But soon it would become clear that the opening of the west, while filling the railroads pockets, had, in fact, ruined the economy.

In a matter of years, the west had become scattered with towns and settlements in various states of development, littered with a disorganized hodge podge of industry and commerce. Now, it was rapidly filling up with gold and silver and felled timber with no place to go, no jewelers to transform nuggets into necklaces, and no ladies to purchase those necklaces to be worn at social events. And even if you could fill the trains with lumber and produce going east, what about the empty trains going west? Just how much lumber could the population of the United States consume? With overproduction came a predictable and steep drop in prices; the whole thing collapsed. Those ordinary citizens, those dupes lured by God and gold, who had hung in there and fought an unnamed and vicious war for the sake of staked claims in hard country, finally started to give it up. Busted, remaining homesteaders and grubstakers started turning over their land and prospects to anyone who was buying—which the corporations weren't anymore. The corporations had fed on free land, investment capital, and the raw materials gleaned from their land rights for so long they had nearly forgotten that at some point they would have to actually earn their money. When that time came, the economy was so bloated there was no possible way for the population to consume all of what was being produced on land west of the Missouri. Combine that with the cost of the war and ongoing reconstruction, and by the end of the nineteenth century, the country was entrenched in a worsening depression.

Somebody had to get control over the beast.

The federal government decided that it would be the adult in the room. At first that was just fine with the corporations. They didn't need to own all of that land anymore, not now that they were beginning to run out of ways to exploit it and all the easy diggings were gone. So, they took all that private land they had acquired off those settlers they had suckered and what they had been gifted by Uncle Sam and handed it right back to the federal government It was clear that it needed to be regulated, but how?

Maybe, the conjecture was, the solution lay in the west itself. Maybe filling it with people and creating an economy of consumption could fix the problem of overabundance. Only, it didn't seem like anyone was interested anymore. The railroad had already made it possible for people to reach the west coast from the east in just a few days of relatively comfortable travel, and still they had not come. Even after the war, with all the mess of reconstruction and all the relocation that came with it, Americans mostly lived in the east and seemed to like it that way. Moreover, they weren't interested in living in the wilderness, whatever ideals or beliefs were attached to it. Americans were moving out of the countryside into cities at incredible rates. The vast expanse of nature in the west was not calling to them. So, the solution would not, could not, at least for some time, be permanent residents. It would have to be visitors or potential investors, maybe. Tourists. To do and see what though? The flatness of the plains? The greenness of the trees? The deepness of the canyons? Yes. It would have to be. There wasn't anything else.

Like Marcus Whitman, or the early colonial promoters, the powers that be realized that a little propaganda could go a long way. Ad campaigns would be needed. The message would need to capture imaginations and capitalize on the post-war zeitgeist. Americans, weary and wounded from war wanted a new, unified national identity. For that, the propagandizers turned to Durant's vision. They reinvented the west as The West, as a place to play, away from the slums and filthy water of the eastern cities. To do so, they curated nature, capitalizing on those landforms that didn't contain the most precious resources but which were most likely to inspire that sense of ecstatic grace so espoused by the Transcendentalists in the hopes that they could co-opt those feelings and turn them into consumer sentiment.

Come west, they said, to open land, big skies, and rolling prairies. Come west, not to monuments or museums, not to be hidden in the shadows of a theater or forced to bow to the upper elite. Come west and dip your toes in the fantasy of a different world, one without the perils of the city but instead imbued with the thrill of the chase, of the hunt, of discovery, and always the possibility of striking it rich, striking oil, striking gold. Come west to play in unfettered country, free to all of us. Come west and see the expanse of your freedoms as they play across the land. Come west and see heaven waiting for you. Come west to find that most-American of freedoms—opportunity, if only for a weekend, if only as a tourist, if only to spend or dine or shoot a buffalo. Come west, to Indian country without the Indians. Come west.

So the west became a place for play, for recreation and leisure, not for toiling in the dirt and muck. With that cognitive transition came the possibility of purchasing leisure and freedom, which quickly became a part of the American Dream: consumption as a patriotic art form. In 1872 Congress created Yellowstone National Park, the first federally protected national park, and a tribute to the monumental nature of the young country's wilderness—not its culture, academics, or institutions. By 1877, though, the country was in a full-blown depression. The west may have captured the American imagination, but there it would have to stay—no ordinary working people had the money to actually see it for themselves. Almost immediately wilderness, whatever that had come to mean, the landscape itself, and especially public lands, became nearly the sole domain of the elite and rich.

Then, in 1891, mere moments after declaring the frontier closed, Congress passed another land-use law designed to quell the corporate beast, the Forest Reserve Act. It granted the president the right to set aside forests in the public domain as "reserves" for future use. It was sold to the public as a means of protecting watersheds, controlling flooding and erosion, and reining in out-of-control mining and logging operations. To implement this legislation, lawmakers created a bespoke bureaucracy, a tangle of new agencies and departments tasked with various forms of environmental regulation that amounted to a massive reassertion of federal control over the land and how it was used. In the end, it was seen as just another land grab. In the first decade of the Forest Reserve Act alone, Presidents Benjamin Harrison and Grover Cleveland set aside more than 30 million acres to be controlled by the federal government. The corporations howled, but decades of their own corruption and greed stood against them and the feds had finally caught up. If you wanted access to natural resources in the public domain, you were going to have to play by the rules.

The management of those public lands was further codified in 1898, when a Yale-educated young man from a wealthy and politically prominent family named Gifford Pinchot was hired as the head of the Division of Forestry. He was a man of long vision and a believer in the scientific method. More importantly, he was influenced by John Muir, the grandfather of the preservationist movement who had helped create the National Park system. Pinchot, like Muir, believed in preservation, but he also believed in management and use of these lands; a mindset very similar to those early settler notions of stewardship. So, at the turn of the century, as part of preserving these new public lands, he set about instituting regulations over them, which he did liberally, placing new controls on grazing, water rights, and power infrastructure and generation.

This, in many ways, satiated the public, who, with the closing of the frontier, had for the first time begun to see the land and its resources as finite, or even endangered. They were embracing workplace safety, sanitation, and other socialist environmental reforms in urban settings; why not in the wild? The preservation and curation of the nation's land treasures as the National Parks, and the mass nostalgia for The West had created a vision of the wild as Madonna, untouched, pure, and fleeting. The American love affair with The West had coalesced with the federal government's new systems of regulation and management of what were now public lands into a full-fledged movement—American conservationism. Conservationism melded the myth of the frontier—freedom, independence, self-sufficiency, and dominance over land and other peoples with land ownership, control, and gate-kept access. No longer was the west a barren void, or an endless source of undug gold; now it was the source of American spirit itself. To conserve these now cherished places, to hold them and to use them sustainably, was to preserve the American identity. Regulation seemed part and parcel of that conservation.

When the frontier closed in 1890 with the end of most federal homesteading laws, nearly all the tenable land had been fenced, mostly with a new, particularly vicious product, barbed wire. From then on, the open frontier west would exist only as a myth in the hearts of the American public.

Nothing embodied this new American mythology more than Buffalo Bill.

SIGNPOST

After the closing of the frontier, when most Americans thought about The West, they pictured the plains and desert lands to the east of Oregon and California, of mining country, red rocks, and massive trees. Even the dry washes of the Humboldt Sink held a kind of nostalgia. They had almost forgotten why people had gone into the terra incognita in the first place, what the original destination or purpose had been, or that it had ever belonged to anyone but themselves. Once again, the map of The West became a thing of fiction, of spectacle and farce like those old mappae mundi. A lot of that fiction, like that of Christopher Columbus four hundred years earlier, was due to one man—Buffalo Bill.

EIGHT

TRAIL STORY: GRUBSTAKE

Buffalo Bill Cody, for all the myths and tall tales, was the real deal. A second-generation settler born in the years between the Great Migration and the Gold Rush, he was raised in Kansas territory and fought for the north in the Civil War after having enlisted at just seventeen years old. After the war, he picked up a contract supplying buffalo meat to the railroad. He was good at it, very good. In just eighteen months, he killed more than four thousand American bison. He was a true product of and believer in the original myths of the west. It's said that his favorite literary passage was from "Verses on the Prospect of Planting Arts and Learning in America" by George Berkeley, a failed missionary in the earliest American colonies:

The Muse, disgusted at an age and clime
Barren of every glorious theme,
In distant lands now waits a better time,
Producing subjects worthy fame….
Westward the course of empire takes its way

American bison aren't the same thing as the "true" buffalo found in Africa and Asia, but the two terms are almost universally used interchangeably. It's estimated that in the earliest days of westward expansion nearly 60 million bison ranged across nearly all of North America. It wouldn't last. Those numbers would be hunted down to less than five hundred by the end of the century. It seems impossible given their size and power. Ten feet long and weighing upward of one thousand or even two thousand pounds, they travel in herds numbering in the thousands. But even as a dominant species in the landscape by numbers, they are generally benevolent. They spend their days grazing the grasslands and wallowing in shallow depressions in the dirt. Still, they have great powers of self-defense. In addition to being massive, they are unpredictable, agile, and in possession of sharpened horns. They run up to thirty-five miles per hour. In spite of all this, killing one with a firearm is startlingly easy, that is, if you can manage to hit one, a task made no easier from horseback. In the Old West, the hardest parts of killing buffalo were surviving finding them in the first place and transporting the meat back to the buyer. Bill was good at both and it made him famous.

In 1869 a man named Ned Buntline started writing about Bill in serials and major newspapers. His patriotic depiction of Cody resonated with war-weary Americans; they couldn't get enough. Time passed and his popularity grew, but Bill was getting old and needed to find an easier way to make his money. By 1883, nearly fifteen years after Stanford and Durant had failed to drive that golden spike into the ground, uniting the country east to west with the railroad, unity between the north and south still seemed elusive. The country needed a hero just as badly as the economy needed a boost. All of a sudden came Buffalo Bill, middle aged and graying, but still, like the buffalo herd he brought with him, agile and unpredictable. And he was shooting true. With him seemed to be the whole of the frontier, or what was left of it, in a new show called *Buffalo Bill's Wild West.*

In *Buffalo Bill's Wild West* there were "Indian" raids, sharp-shooting events, foot and horse races, reenactments of (loosely interpreted) historical events, hunts, wild animals, including bears performing trained tricks, and one of the last buffalo herds in existence. It was a spectacle nearly four hours in length, a cousin to vaudeville and the circuses of the day. Soon it was so popular they were able to take the tour to Europe. Some of his success was timing.

The age of advertising and mass media was unfolding and *Buffalo Bill's Wild West* was capitalizing on it. Ahead of the travelling show came publicity the likes of which had never been seen before, publicity that relied on mass media—print, radio, telegraph, photography, and some of the first moving film images in history. There were stunts, op-ed articles, celebrity endorsements, organized press kits, billboards. Bill even dabbled in product licensing. Everywhere they went they entered each city or town in a costumed parade with music and marching and men on horseback and wild animals on leashes that stopped traffic and clogged sidewalks with spectators. People loved it. Thousands of them a day, day after day, took in Bill, his Congress of Rough Riders, and what before the end of the century would come to be billed as "The Drama of Civilization." Bill brought The West, with all its fantasies right to the people.

Two years after the government announced the closure of the frontier, the show hit its apex. Millions of people from around the world flocked to see the frontier festival at the Chicago World's Fair, cementing The West forever in their minds. That same year at the fair, Frederick Turner, a young scholar and future Harvard history professor deeply influenced by the works of Emerson and Darwin, gave a speech to the American Historical Association pronouncing, "The frontier is gone, and with its going has closed the first period of American history." Turner believed in evolution and was working with geologists in Wisconsin at the time of his address to apply those principles to the development of the American identity. In his model, the American spirit was founded in the pursuit of western lands, which he defined as a boundary line between civilization and savagery. More than that, Turner argued that the experience of migration and settlement had caused American behavior to evolve into a form of individualism that, mirroring the challenges and harshness of pioneer life, lacked refinement and emphasized individualism. It was a problematic and somewhat offensive view. But that didn't seem to matter, the American people had fallen in love with this new version of themselves, for better or worse.

The Applegates, unlike so many settlers and grubstakers who had made the long journey west, were there for all of it, through the opening and closing of the frontier, the "cowboys and Indians," the sharp shooting. They had lived and breathed every part of *Buffalo Bill's Wild West*, occupying their own trail, more or less, until the closing of the frontier.

That first bitter taste of Oregon Country never faded for the brothers. In an 1848 Way Bill describing the Applegate Route to forthcoming emigrants, Jesse warns new arrivals to ensure they retain a milk cow to the end of the journey as, he said, "*the people here are poor and hard hearted.*" But they persisted. At first, Lindsay joined the gold rush, but found the conditions too harsh and returned home, losing most of his lode to grifters and sour deals along the way. Then, he and Jesse had thought they could capitalize on the gold rush the easy way, by selling supplies to miners headed out to the claims and converting their golden nuggets into watches and jewelry ready for the eastern market as they came back in. Value-added products, they reasoned, were where the real money was. As Susan Applegate describes, they put up the first building at the base of the mining hills in the Rogue valley. It immediately drew prospectors and passers by setting out for their claims. All those wagons and white men drew the attention of the Rogue Indians, who had for some time been locked in a war with the federal government, and settlers as its proxy, over their territory. They made it clear the Applegates and their building were unwelcome. The status quo was to dig in and hold the land, but the brothers couldn't stomach it. When the time came and, as Susan Applegate puts it, "arrows were flying past their hats," they made a run for it back up the valley to their families, burning their fort behind them. As a brutally ironic end to the incident, they spied their first potential customer, a returning miner, on a ridgetop above them as they fled north toward Charles's homestead in the Yoncalla Valley.

After that, it seemed like Jesse and Lindsay were always doing something new. Lindsay stayed close to his family for a time, operating a toll road for a time, participating in county politics, and, never forgetting that first year's tragedy, serving as the captain of a volunteer company that protected incoming emigrants along the southern routes.

But the brothers had itchy feet and spent large amounts of time away from their families. Eventually, Lindsay joined the army, hunting down deserters. When he returned, he moved his family away from his brother's homesteads in the Willamette valley and reestablished himself near present day Ashland. There, he served as a Special Indian Agent during the Rogue wars, and proved himself to be a leader like his brother, commanding his own company. Even with his absences, he and his wife Elizabeth had twelve children together, five of whom would die before their parents, taken by the hardships of Oregon Country.

Even with the damage done to his reputation by the southern road debacle, Jesse stayed in politics, becoming a member of the government commission charged with settling the territorial dispute. When the issue of Oregon's Territory's borders was finally settled, he focused his attentions closer to home, that led to him becoming active in the political affairs in southern Oregon, serving as a justice of the peace, and establishing his house in Yoncalla as an official polling location and post office. For a time, he and Cynthia even ran a general store out of the building. They had at least twelve children as well, though half did not make it to the next century and at least two were lost as infants.

For the most part, Jesse's reputation seemed restored. He was known for maintaining a massive private library and well respected for his prolific writing, which covered topics from the political to the personal. It even earned him a new nickname, "the Sage of Yoncalla." But he was dogged by misfortune. He lost his house and land claim by unwittingly backing an embezzling friend in a government bonds scandal. When his friend's scheme was discovered, the courts held him liable in a decision that left him deep in debt. After that, he ran cattle with first his sons and then his grandsons on someone else's seventy thousand acres of privately held, consolidated land until the debt could be repaid. Then, against all of his moral directives, one of his daughters married a southern sympathizer. Unable to tolerate their perspective, he disowned her, a loss he felt as a death. At the end of his life, he is said to have paced the floors at night, unable to sleep, reportedly terrorized by visions of death and people he had lost passed.

Charles had brokered a tenuous peace with the Indigenous inhabitants who had used the valley for centuries to harvest and process camas root and they allowed him to reside there as a farmer without fear of violence. There, he constructed a two story, white-washed home with ample porches and low interior ceilings. It quickly became a cornerstone of the rapidly growing community, in spite of its unusual layout. Charles, not known for teetotalling, had nonetheless constructed it as two separate living spaces, one for himself and the other men of the family, and one for his wife and daughters. There was no interior passage; if Melinda wanted to speak to her husband, she had to exit her side and enter through his exterior door like any other visitor. Whether this arrangement was her idea or his, no one has ever known. Still, it stood impressively against the landscape.

Oregon Country never produced the bounty the brothers had been promised in Missouri and what successes they did have were often balanced by floods, illness, and the changing population and political landscape. Yoncalla never became a city, nor did any of the nearby settlements. Toward the end of their lives, Lindsay moved his family away and the distance and busyness of life caused the brothers to grow apart. Charles died on August 9, 1879, leaving his wife Melinda and twelve of their sixteen children to chart their own routes through Oregon Country.

None of the brothers would live to see what was to come of Oregon Country or their southern emigrant route. Jesse died nine years after Charles, and Lindsay followed him a few years after that, in 1892, just as the frontier closed. Their legacy though, endures. The house Charles built is still standing. It is considered one of the oldest homes in Oregon and was continuously occupied by his descendants into the twenty-first century. The controversy surrounding the southern road and their role in the tragic events of that first year hounded them to the end of their lives. It too, carried on into the twenty-first century with descendants on all sides still fighting over who's name deserves to be attached to the trail.

NINE

THE MARRIAGE OF WAR AND PROSPERITY, 1891–1945

CONSERVATION AS IT WAS CREATED, PACKAGED, AND SOLD BY heads of government agencies like the Forest Service or, in 1916, the new National Parks Service, had turned out pretty well for the government. At heart, Pinchot had proved to be a businessman. And while he aligned his values with the likes of Muir and Emerson, who believed that wilderness should remain untouched by the hand of man, Pinchot believed in working land and working forests. More than that, he believed that U.S. forestland could be a source of wealth and that the government could, and should, foster the sustained procurement of that wealth. The public largely believed the line that the west's lands and resources were owned by all (white people) and were being protected and preserved, largely untouched, as a symbol of unbridled American freedom (for white people). Instead, they were being systematically parsed, exploited, controlled, and sold by the government, right down to the water flowing silently under the ground, the rock itself, and the rails stapled into it. Conservation, as opposed to strict preservation, had been pushed at the public by powerful men and corporations that wanted a share of Pinchot's promised wealth. It was another land grab, only this time made by the government. In many ways, conservation was just a mechanism of distraction from that grab.

Recreation programs and the National Parks directed the public's attention away from the land grab, and into a new American fantasy rooted in those now idealized notions of freedom, self-reliance, and adventure being perpetuated by mass media. In the curated wilderness of the conservation era, Americans could play and rest or even seek that elusive ecstatic grace; meanwhile, the government could set about regulating resources and consumption and, most importantly, setting the United States up to enter the global economy, which needed to happen to turn the flailing economy around.

On maps, political boundaries and capitals are always boldly marked. In many cases, what lies beyond those boundaries is depicted as a void. These political boundaries are the hardest edges of the maps, the least malleable and most difficult to cross in real life. They come loaded with massive shifts in culture, commerce, language, and religion. What sits in the middle of the map is the thing of most import—everything else is marginalized. In the World War era, the center of the map was considered up for grabs, and the United States was determined to stake a claim. The still-fledgling country, though, would have to do so by force.

Defensively speaking, the geographic advantage was obvious. The United States had no interest in resuming fighting with European nations and more land was not what they needed. Trade was what the country needed. War meant more exports and more exports meant more production. It was the same problem they had tried to fix with the railroads. What to do with all the excess and abundance from all that land and all those people and how to turn it into gold. So, war, the bigger the better. It would be good for business. Theodore Roosevelt had seen the need for it even before being elected to office, writing in 1897: "In strict confidence…I should welcome almost any war, for I think this country needs one."

The State Department, Howard Zinn aptly points out in his history of the United States, agreed, writing just one year later: "It seems to be conceded that every year we shall be confronted with an increasing surplus of manufactured goods for sale in foreign markets if American operatives and artisans are to be kept employed the year around. The enlargement of foreign consumption of the products of our mills and workshops has, therefore, become a serious problem of statesmanship as well as of commerce."

But the turn of the century came and went without incident. The country matured and agencies grew and regulations blossomed. The American public, insulated by distance, celebrated itself, its innovation, progress, and modernization. "The West" as a vehicle for escapism and entertainment was bigger than ever before, but interest in live shows waned as movies began to take over. In 1913 *Buffalo Bill's Wild West* show was declared bankrupt. The next year the Archduke of Austria, Franz Ferdinand was assassinated. War had arrived and, as historian Richard Hofstadter would later describe, "America became bound up with the Allies in a fateful union of war and prosperity."

Patriotic, not religious spirit, would define this new century.

The war, as expected, was great for the economy. Manufacturing did indeed boom, along with communications and a host of other industries. Not everyone benefitted equally. The upper class fared far better than the working class who had no means of increasing their piece of the new pie. The pie seemed to get smaller all the time as millions of new immigrants poured into the country. Like the Donner party, Americans turned on one another.

They also turned against science, particularly where it intersected with issues of social justice. Darwinism was banned in schools. The Scopes Monkey Trial took place. Pseudo sciences like astrology and divination gained popularity. Moral judgement seemed to be of high importance with prohibition being passed in 1920, but morality did not. That year, an estimated 2 million Americans, were members of the Ku Klux Klan.

There were other signs of changing times. The national birthrate was low, the death rate was too. Environmental reforms had taken effect; homes were insulated and well heated, workplaces were safer, and more people had access to refrigeration, sanitation, and clean drinking water. Women were allowed to vote. Black Americans were not. Modernism had arrived and with it, urbanization; nearly half the country now lived in cities. World War I ended, and American culture roared for better or worse into the 1920s, dragging these contradictions and problems with it.

Then the stock market crashed, destroying the economy. People lost jobs. Farm income decreased nearly fifty percent. Corporations suffered too, but while banks were bailed out, the average American was not. Unemployment rose to thirty percent or more, and spirits sagged as Americans brought up on the rhetoric of brave self-sufficiency found themselves on skid row, forcibly idle, waiting in bread lines. Alcoholism, drug addiction, and depression rose. Americans cast about, looking for someone to blame. Like the Applegates in the heated moments after the loss of their sons, they lashed out at whomever was near, whomever was different. Laws were enacted restricting immigration, preventing people of Japanese or Chinese descent from owning property or leasing land.

And the sun shone and the wind blew and all that land in between the great cities dried out. Wells ran dry. Fields refused to yield. And when the crops were gone and the land was bare, the wind came and stole the soil from all the homesteads that had been so righteously claimed some eighty years earlier.

Hope didn't return until the election of Franklin D. Roosevelt in 1932 and the implementation of his grandest idea, the New Deal. It was a plan of economic rejuvenation, sure, but at the core of his New Deal was the revitalization of the patriotic, pastoral American landscape. He, like Pinchot, believed that the United States' true wealth lay in the use and exploitation of its lands and resources. Like Humboldt, he understood that mismanagement could, and had, led to disaster. In his inaugural address, from the depths of the Dust Bowl, he placed hope on the promise of the land:

> Only a foolish optimist can deny the dark realities of the moment. Yet our distress comes from no failure of substance. We are stricken by no plague of locusts. Compared with the perils which our forefathers conquered because they believed and were not afraid, we have still much to be thankful for. Nature still offers her bounty and human efforts have multiplied it. Plenty is at our doorstep, but a generous use of it languishes in the very sight of the supply.

Roosevelt went on to lay out an ambitious plan to restore the "temple of our civilization." It would require more than government subsidies, he warned. It would take the labor of the masses, mobilized as a "trained and loyal army" and invested into the earth itself, what he called "a recognition of the old and permanently important manifestation of the American spirit of the pioneer."

In Roosevelt's New Deal, that spirit of the pioneer, was manifested in the control of nature, in civic projects, dams, highways, and roads and in the facing and deterring of fears; precursors to the Federal Emergency Management Agency (FEMA) were established, as were farm aid and the rural electrification program. Gone was the "soft manhood" of the urban American, decried by the first Roosevelt. It was replaced by the new icon of the economic recovery—the Civilian Conservation corpsman, rough riders for a new age.

The Civilian Conservation Corps (CCC) was meant to rally the men of America out of the depression and into action. Literally. The program offered work in the form of hard labor, often in harsh terrain. It wasn't an entirely new idea. The wealth of the United States had always been gleaned from the land, usually with forced and indentured labor. Three decades into the twentieth century, with nearly every township and range box occupied, slavery abolished, and labor rights and unions in place, that work now needed to be done by the average person. If only they could be coaxed to take up the tasks, reeducated, as it were. Where better than the vast spaces of the American West for that reeducation to play out? Everyone knew that was where "real men" were made, look at Buffalo Bill. The Civilian Conservation Corps sent 300,000 men to work in forest camps, planting trees, building reservoirs and dams, constructing bridges and fire towers, clearing out diseased and invasive plants, building campgrounds and roads, and generally putting the American West, what portions of it could still be considered untamed, firmly under the thumb of man's modern engineering. It was conservationism at work. For nine years they did all that and more, building forest camps, implementing soil-erosion programs, and putting in hiking trails and recreation facilities. All told, it's estimated that they planted more than 3 billion trees. More than seven hundred new state parks were created as part of the program.

These "new men," sometimes called Roosevelt's Tree Army, lived and worked in a military style, which was handy. Fascism was on the rise everywhere, but Americans would stay focused on their troubles at home until the 1941 attack on Pearl Harbor. Then, the program was used as a resource for soldiers and their encampments as military infrastructure. Roosevelt's New Deal had laid the plans for America to become a world power once they entered the war, which is exactly what happened. When the attack came, it was an affront, particularly coming as it did from the west, and in doing so, threatening such symbolic country. It was clear a tipping point had been reached. There would be no staying out of the war.

When United States forces formally entered the conflict, they did so under a banner of humanitarian righteousness. But the real goal of American involvement in the war was the same as it had always been, long-term economic stability at home, an exportation fix for the domestic overproduction problem that had plagued the country ever since the opening of the frontier. The fix would not come easily, requiring sacrifices and changes in behavior from every citizen. Americans adopted a conservation mentality and shifted their relationship to the natural world and its derivatives. There were victory gardens and state propaganda urged the reduction of household food waste, reuse of goods, and the value of mending. There were recycling initiatives and ride-sharing programs designed to conserve metals, rubber, and gasoline for the military. Even household waste fats from cooking were collected for the war effort as such fats were needed for the production of glycerin, an essential component of American bombs.

Production exploded across nearly every industry. By 1941 lumber was the major industry in Lane County, Oregon, the northernmost extent of the Applegate Trail. And in the coming years it would reach record levels as the industry stretched to meet the needs of national defense. Across the Applegate Trail, cities shifted gears. Coos Bay built more warships than fisheries; Nevada became a nuclear testing ground. In this instance, the trickle-down theory of economics worked—as long as the war kept going. The massive numbers of men being recruited or drafted into the armed services led to opportunity for those groups typically left out of the workforce (women) and those traditionally undervalued (people of color). As long as the trees kept falling and the factories kept producing, the war could create wealth for nearly every American.

Before that prosperity arrived, sacrifice touched nearly every part of American life. In 1942 the metal rails on Promontory Summit were salvaged as part of the war effort. Hardly anyone noticed, though nostalgic locals participated in a ceremonial "undriving" of the last spike. Even it was no longer golden, having been replaced shortly after the completion ceremony. That same year, the National War Labor Board closed the gold mines and made gold mining illegal. The economy peaked in January 1945. The war ended just nine months later. When it did, powerful men once again sat down to rewrite the mappae mundi. This time, America took center place.

SIGNPOST

There is no understating the importance of the railroads to the growth of the United States and its people's relationship to the land, its resources and cultivation. While still essential even today, railroads had in many respects gone the way of the dinosaurs by the end of World War II. The railroads' diminished role in the public consciousness did little to heal the damage that was done during their installation.

TEN

TRAIL STORY: *THE GENERAL*

"I took that page of history, and I stuck to it in all detail. I staged it exactly the way it happened."
—BUSTER KEATON, ON *THE GENERAL*

A SLIM FIGURE RUNS AT BREAKNECK SPEED DOWN A NARROW track toward the back of an old steam locomotive engine. Music plays furiously in the background as a piano pumps out a kind of frantic polyphonic ragtime. The runner catches up, his puffed shirt sleeves and long-stringed western tie ruffling like feathers in the breeze as he reaches up and leaps toward the ladder down the back of the runaway engine. He catches it with both hands, one foot landing lightly on the narrow rest, the other coming behind at the ankle, elegantly pointed like a dancer crossed in fifth.

The man makes his way to the front of the engine and climbs atop its cab. For a moment he leans inhumanly forward into the wind, one hand shielding his eyes from the sun, while behind him in the distance massive conifers zoom past. Ahead of him on the tracks a group of Union soldiers drop railroad ties across the track in an effort to derail him. He spots the hazard, frowns, and furrows his brow. Then he dashes forward along the roof and makes his way down the snout of the engine to the cowcatcher. There, he manages to pull the tie off the tracks just in the nick of time, and for a moment he rests back against the massive train car, legs splayed out in front of him, skimming over the track.

The man was Buster Keaton, and the movie was perhaps 1927's biggest failure, *The General.*

Keaton, born Joseph Frank Keaton just before the turn of the twentieth century, worked his way to stardom in the silent film industry after decades on the road with his family on the Vaudeville circuit. On screen, he was solemn faced, with high cheekbones, the hollows accentuated by makeup and a mop of dark curls under a porkpie hat—an ordinary guy, caught in the struggles of everyday life. He was lean, agile, detail oriented, and never cracked a smile. People loved him for it; he was the hero of the everyman's melancholy.

In person, he was a genius and a madman, a clown and a true vaudevillian, with pitch-perfect timing and always, always, ready to take the drop. He was famous for elaborate stunts, filming them himself with no safety precautions, usually in real situations. For *The General*, he pushed this tendency to the limits, riding astride real steam engines and ordering the crew to keep filming until he called cut or was dead.

It seemed he couldn't help himself. He worked that movie like a man possessed from the beginning, jumping at the chance to make the story, which he derived from a Civil War memoir entitled *The Great Locomotive Chase*. It's a story about love, theft, and subterfuge in the final days of the Civil War, but mostly it's a story about train chases and heroism as one brave man fights to "save his two great loves": a girl, and a steam engine named The General.

The book tells the true story of the only locomotive chase of the war. In 1862 a Union regiment stole a Confederate passenger train named The General in an attempt to prevent it from delivering supplies. Southern trains chased them as the Union soldiers tried to get away by destroying the track behind them, pulling out telegraph wires, and even trying to burn a railroad bridge after crossing. It didn't work. Confederate troops eventually recaptured The General and executed the soldiers, but the Union considered the damage to the southern army's supply chain a win.

Right away, Keaton knew it was too big a story to film in a studio. It had to be authentic. Keaton loved trains, and he envisioned using them to turn what could easily have been a romantic comedy into a high drama. "The slapstick stuff is gone," he said. "The movie public demands drama, punctuated with comedy." It was a tough order, but if anyone was up to the challenge it was Keaton. Like Buffalo Bill, his was a world of dancing girls and flying families, where men shot out of canons and the tiniest of dancers tamed elephants. Part circus, part theater, Vaudeville was an entertainment for the masses, an immigrant's diversion that reveled in the tragic and the absurd. Keaton thought he understood those masses. To him, the Civil War, reflected them.

It should have been perfect. And maybe it would have been, except for Keaton's own tragic absurdity. Keaton was a southern sympathizer and he believed that the hearts and spirit of true America, the moviegoing public, agreed with him. He truly thought that no mainstream American audience could ever view the south as the villains they were. So, he flipped the narrative and created a truth-denying version of the events that cast the

Confederacy as the triumphant underdogs and the north as the Union aggressors.

He ran into pushback almost immediately. At the time, the south was going through something of a reckoning, attempting to expel the most visible ranks of the KKK from its territory and driving the rest underground. Written as a confederate revisionist piece, he couldn't find a location in the south that was willing to allow him to film *The General.*

Then in April 1926, the movie's location manager found a small town in what could fairly be described as the middle of nowhere Oregon that boasted more covered bridges than any other place west of the Mississippi and plenty of old rail lines. Cottage Grove was an old mining town situated at the upper end of the Willamette Valley where the valley floor rises and the foothills of the Cascade Mountains begin to converge with the rumpled ridgelines of the coast range and the Klamath Mountains. The town itself is floodplain flat, lying at the confluence of the Row River and the coast fork of the Willamette River, but around it on all sides are steep forested slopes. The Applegates had noted the imposing beauty of the area, the contrast of the surrounding high mountains with the gently sloped arable valleys below, on their pathfinding mission; both Jesse and Charles had made their homesteads just twenty-five miles to the south. It would be perfect for *The General.*

It helped that the town looked decades behind the rest of the world, a consequence of its never having really been a place. Its modern history mirrored most of the rest of the west. It was founded as a roadside stop, a collection point for mail, minerals (gold had been found in some of those knobby hills), and lumber along the Applegate Trail. It was a population center based on convenience, and perhaps for that reason had never made much of itself. Like most everywhere else, the gold had run dry in the mines, so the last remaining industry was timber, and even that was fading. Now, war was driving the economy. The same year that Keaton set eyes on Cottage Grove, the railroads, in a reversal of their land-grabbing grifts of the 1800s, declared that their easement land was worth more as agricultural land than for timber, and the federal government opened the land back up for homesteading, with World War I veterans at the front of the line. With so little modern infrastructure and that stunning landscape, Keaton thought he would be able to re-create the old south with relative ease.

There was one other great advantage for Keaton. There, neither his bravado nor his content would cause alarm. Indeed, the bravado, in a land of lumberjacks, miners, and military men was welcome. So, surprisingly, was the Confederate sympathy. But why?

Because even though the Civil War ended slavery nearly before Oregon became a state, even though the Oregon Territory had not endorsed slavery, even though no battles had been fought within its boundaries, the issue of slavery and most particularly the racism that enabled it, was written just as deeply into the soil and face of Oregon Country as the scars from mining and timber or the sutures of the railroad. Oregon was an exclusion state. Black people were not allowed to live or work within the territory under a system that promised violent recourse. The railroads played a starring role in the implementation of these policies, resulting in a practice that would hasten the decline of new towns and hamper population growth well into the twentieth century. For decades after the arrival of the railroad Black employees were not allowed off the trains, forcing them to pass on through. By the 1920s, Oregon was notably white. Under pressure in the south, the Klan noticed, and in 1921 its members began to migrate there, soon making the area surrounding Cottage Grove part of its new nexus. In this whites-only no place, Keaton would receive no pushback from the locals over *The General*'s revisionist storyline. So west he went, to Oregon Country. And indeed, the people there loved him, especially when he proved to be far more personable than his dour onscreen façade, a look which had garnered him the nickname, the Great Stone Face.

Keaton arrived in Cottage Grove the same way Buffalo Bill would have and as the emigrant wagon trains did—as a caravan of players: actors, cooks, and crew that brought with them everything they could possibly need, from costumes to cannons and cameras and their own locomotives, stagecoaches, and wagons. Keaton even bought his own chef to prepare meals for the crew. For Cottage Grove, it was a bonanza. The film hired more than fifteen hundred locals—nearly the entirety of the town, to stand in as extras, which they did with glee. For months nearly everything else ground to a halt. The crew transformed the city and the land around it to recreate the town of Marietta Georgia, complete with false-fronted hotels, barrooms, and train depots and Oregon's languishing timber as the backdrop. During the days, they filmed. In the evenings they organized cookouts and baseball games and even an improvised vaudeville show, all featuring Keaton in a starring role. "Keaton fishes and plays ball with the same energy that he puts into the making of a picture," a local paper commented. "He is the star of his team…nimble and alert."

The games were an important counterpoint to an otherwise grueling work schedule made worse by the relentless heat of a record-breaking summer. While Cottage Grove had the type of vintage tracks needed for the film, there was only one-half mile of parallel lines on which to film shots of Keaton on the locomotive or running along the tracks. To make an entire sequence, viewed from several angles, Keaton had to stitch together tiny segments of the action, moving everything—actors and cameras and props and backgrounds—back to the start and setting up again, over and over, day after day, week after week.

Eventually, the area became so tinder dry from the heat wave that sparks from the old engines set fire to nearby haystacks up Culp Creek, which in turn, set the surrounding forest on fire. Keaton was said to have leaped into action to direct the fight as did the more than five hundred Oregon State Guardsmen the governor had loaned him for the shoot. When the fire was brought under control, Keaton was heralded as a hero and the governor awarded him an honorary captaincy.

The incident didn't stop Keaton from playing with fire. In fact, the final shot of the film depended on it. That day people from around the county gathered, excused from work by general consent and the unofficial decree of a local holiday to witness the demolition by fire of a train trestle constructed specifically for the scene into the Row River. Keaton had invested more than $40,000 in the stunt and had only one chance to get it right, which he did. The train, ordered to cross already burning tracks by an inept Union commander, buckles from the center as it passes over the flames, disappearing entirely into the water as cavalrymen and foot soldiers begin to ford the river. From the bank, the dumbstruck commander stares stupidly at the collapsed track before ordering his men to continue advancing. But on the other bank, Confederate soldiers lie in wait, ultimately outgunning the

Union soldiers as they struggle to cross the river, forcing them to retreat as strains of "Dixie" play through the smoke. Eventually, a rogue cannonball launched by an incompetent Keaton finds its way to the nearby dam, unleashing a flood of water on the remaining Union soldiers. The battle is won, the supply train is disabled, and Keaton stands proudly with the Confederate flag on a rock overlooking the valley.

After the final railroad scene was shot, Keaton left Cottage Grove as the hero of a triumphant Confederate south, at least in his own mind. The production company left the discarded remains of *The General* in the Row River. Outside of Lane County, the movie drew terrible critical reviews, a flop at the box office and morally (nobody had a sense of humor about the Civil War, and many questioned the wisdom of finding one), and it marked the end of the silent film era. Keaton, who had so badly misread the hearts of the American people, went down with it, first losing artistic control of his future projects, then descending into addiction and, finally, madness. At one point he escaped from a straitjacket while institutionalized using the skills he had learned from his days on the circuit with Houdini. The General remained in the Row River for over a decade, serving as a kind of quirky roadside attraction until 1944, when it was salvaged for scrap metal as part of the war effort. The public let their memory of Keaton and the Klan, which had disappeared from public view during the Great Depression, fade until nearly forgotten.

Today, the Cottage Grove Hotel still stands, along with many of the other buildings along Main Street that were there during the filming of *The General.* Time has been kind to its memory and forgiving of its revisionist storyline. Critics now see it as an early masterpiece of cinematic stuntsmanship. And Orson Welles once called it the greatest Civil War film ever made, perhaps the greatest film ever made. Now, visitors are welcomed by a decorative arch commemorating the Historic Downtown. To the left of the arch, painted across the brick side of the hotel, is a mural of Keaton, frozen in time, riding the cowcatcher down the rails, eyes wide with determination and alarm, staring down the track.

ELEVEN

PLASTIC FANTASTIC, 1945–1967

JUST AS LINES OF LATITUDE AND LONGITUDE, OR TOWNSHIP and range, act as reference points for the measurement of space, geologic epochs act as reference points for the measurement of time. In math, time is conceptualized as a third-dimensional axis, one of x, y, or z. On maps, time is depicted as the two-dimensional surface expression of geologic layers, units whose spatial relationships at depth providc us with relative temporal information; at the most basic level, old rocks underlie young rocks. Human epochs are defined by trends in culture or historical events, what we term an "epoch event." Similarly, geologic epochs are defined by unique but widespread rock layers, deposits from singular events such as volcanic eruptions or glacial flooding, or the presence of fossils of ubiquitous but short-lived species. We call these layers marker beds, and the characteristics themselves, markers.

Our current epoch, the Holocene, began a little over 11,000 years ago, at the end of the last global ice age when ice sheets as thick as 12,000 feet had covered continents. In North America these sheets moved south across the plains, creating the basins for the Great Lakes and filling the Pacific Northwest with enough ice to create a depression in the crust so great that it now serves as a massive shallow coastal sea, Puget Sound. The cold peaked 18,000 years ago, gradually waning until the climate stabilized at the beginning of the Holocene. Humanity, then, has always existed in a warming world. With this knowledge, one could look at the period of the past 10,000 years, the period humanity associates itself with, as one of an unveiling and revelation, as the cover of ice was lifted from the world and the population spread out and investigated.

Maybe this experience of unveiling seeped into human consciousness as a primary way of coming to know a place. Certainly, it could be said of colonial people in America for whom terrestrial newness held such fascination. That newness, and the quest for newness, were possessions coveted like gold, new land, new ways of doing, new industries, new lives. It seems appropriate then that the word *Holocene* derives from the ancient Greek words *holos*, "wholly," and *kainos*, "new." Much like the United States at its inception, the Holocene represents the newest layer of rocks in the record, the last thing to be lain down and the most likely to be exposed, altered, and degraded. As a consequence, the rocks of the Holocene are defined in some ways by their newness, the nature of their surface expression. The same is true for Americans. This sense of and love for newness has always been a fundamental part of Americanism, one of the tenets of American culture and life ways, and the thing that has perhaps been held most precious in American identity as depicted in the frontier myth.

It was something altogether new that ended World War II, thrusting the United States to the center of the map, and beginning what many scientists argue is a new epoch not just for humanity, but in the geologic record: the Anthropocene, the age of man. It is still a matter of some debate, as the geologists who might determine such matters discuss what, if any, impact generated by humanity on the rock record is sufficiently unique, widespread, and durable over geologic time to constitute a true marker. In discussion, they often refer to this essential marker for which they search as "the golden spike." Some argue it manifests as the human-generated radioactive isotopes, cesium-137, and plutonium-239 and -240, the nuclear isotopes.

The first detonation of a nuclear device happened in a remote desert location in New Mexico on July 16, 1945. The explosion released 18.6 kilotons of power, putting off enough light to illuminate the morning sky many times brighter than the sun, and enough heat to turn the desert sands to glass. At the time, Germany had already surrendered, effectively ending the European war. But Japan refused to yield, locking the United States into a prolonged and deadly sea-based battle for the islands. On the morning of August 6, "Little Boy" was dropped on Hiroshima. It produced a 900-foot-wide fireball that heated the air to over 9,000 degrees. Buildings melted. Organic matter of all kinds—trees, grass, human flesh—vaporized. Eighty thousand people died in an instant, more than 100,000 died in the following months. The total death toll remains unknown. Afterward, President Harry S. Truman released a statement, saying simply: "Sixteen hours ago an American airplane dropped one bomb on Hiroshima and destroyed its usefulness to the enemy.... If they do not now accept our terms, they may expect a rain of ruin from the air, the like of which has never been seen on this earth." He made good on the threat three days later when another bomb was dropped on Nagasaki. That time, Truman drew on American's most base colonial instincts to put a fine point on the moment, saying of the Japanese, "When you have to deal with a beast, you have to treat him as a beast."

The bombs won the war, but forever damaged the soul of the nation. Undeterred by the human and environmental horrors wrought by these new weapons, the United States entered a period of research and proliferation that would grip the world in an altogether different kind of icy hold for decades to come. The first test of an airdropped nuclear device on American land took place six years later, on a dry lakebed in Nevada south of the Humboldt Sink. Over the next decade, 928 such tests, many of them underground, would be conducted at Nevada's test sites, each dispersing radioactive fallout. The nuclear age had arrived.

America came out of World War II a hero, especially in its own mind. Having taken center stage by shock and awe and with little tangible impact on the homeland, Americans set about enjoying the fruits of their wartime economy and Roosevelt's New Deal. Claiming less than ten percent of the world's people, the United States now controlled a majority of the global economy. With that money, the government launched the most expensive affirmative action program the country had ever seen, easily dwarfing the New Deal. The Servicemen's Readjustment Act (G.I. Bill) established a broad array of government benefits including veteran's hospitals and unemployment benefits and provided funding for tuition and housing to more than 9 million servicemen. It was a boon, but not everyone was brought along. The federal government had ended the Japanese internment with the end of the war, but nothing was done to compensate these citizens for their trauma, lost income, or sacrifices for their country. And there were layoffs as defense industries collapsed, creating a cascading economic slump that impacted everything down to resource extraction.

Women and people of color, especially Black Americans, rarely benefitted from the post-war government incentives. Even so, out of the first Roosevelt's vision of prosperity through war arose the great American midcentury middle class.

Quality of life skyrocketed. This new middle class had income, infrastructure, and innovation, and they used it. They had new appliances, medicines, and other modern conveniences like commercial air travel and self-cleaning houses. Newly equipped with affordable, American-made cars built using the steel that once went to railroad tracks, they worked pensioned union jobs with federal safety oversights during the week and played in the new lakes and campgrounds provided by CCC labor and the Army Corps of Engineers on the weekends. Mass production arrived to every sector of the economy, including babies. There were so many babies that the whims and desires of this new predominantly white middle class and their children would dominate the public discourse and economy for the next seventy years. But in the first few years after the wars, all those babies mostly meant America needed a whole lot of houses. So many, in fact, that wood-frame houses seemed to become the new homestead plot—everyone could, and would, have one.

To make it so, the country drank in trees. This was great for the timber companies who had steadfastly taken advantage of each decline in the economy to purchase land and timber tracts at bargain prices, only to sell the lumber later at a premium. Most of the trees came from along the Applegate Trail, where logging became the new mining. Oregon had become the leading timber-producing state in the country in 1937 and would hold that status until 1987, peaking in 1952. But trees, like land or gold, proved to be finite. And there was a technical issue: For more than a hundred years, all the logs had been old growth, but now those massive trees were running out, and because the machinery in the mills had been designed for those massive logs, smaller second-growth trees couldn't be processed. Because of choices made during mechanization, timber, by definition, had to come from old growth. Under pressure from all those babies, timber companies turned to the Forest Service and public lands in search of bigger trunks. The Forest Service, still dedicated to Pinchot's vision of abundance through measured management, acquiesced and began to open increasingly large tracts of old-growth trees to private logging. The west was being sold. Again.

It wasn't just about trees. All those cars needed roads. The Federal-Aid Highway Act of 1944 expanded the Federal Aid Road Act of 1916, which had established the first federal highway system. Freeways became the new railroad. More than 40,000 new highway miles were proposed in the Act to connect cities with the country's growing industrial centers. Additional roads were planned as connectors for the population to access the highways and across public forest lands and National Parks. And there would be, of course, even more infrastructure needed for the associated rest stops, gas stations, newfangled fast-food restaurants, and sundry roadside attractions that would surely follow. The result was a hardscaping of the land surface, especially in cities and in the west where dusty roads and quagmires still ruled, hobbling modernization. Soon, vast ribbons of pavement cut across the country, reaching out through the mountains. Automobiles, land boats, really, complete with fins and built to last, filled the brand-new highways. The oil and gas industries boomed in response, transporting black gold through man-made veins, sucked out and pumped through pipelines across the country.

Like the Hell on Wheels towns of the railroad era, development closely followed the interstates, making each exchange and connection point a hub of commercial and eventually residential development. Migration away from the rural, pastoral landscape intensified as these new corridors began to populate. While previously dispersed populations converged near the cities, industrial parks increasingly ringed them. Soon the landscape was spotted with sprawling shopping malls surrounded by seas of asphalt parking. Midcentury America heralded the coming of an age of peace and American supremacy with the rise of a kitschy consumer culture dominated by visual media. Across the country, people migrated into cities and suburbs in search of the good life. For the first time more Americans described themselves as urban rather than rural.

The American relationship to the environment shifted too, as increased controls were implemented. Electric lighting took over, municipal water systems and sewer systems were installed. Daily life, for many Americans, ceased to be connected to the natural world. Nature, to the nuclear family, was now a consumable in the form of raw material for manufactured goods and curated outdoor spaces for leisure tourism and visual spectacles. The nuclear age also came with a change of aesthetic. Lines were clean and surfaces shiny, new buildings favored banks of windows and open spaces. It was a time of innovation and modernization, which carried with it an ethos of capitalism, materialism, and freedom through consumption. That ethos was reflected in nearly every aspect of life, even the buildings, which used new and modern building materials like Formica, and were built to accommodate the new car-based culture. Everywhere, parking lots paved paradises.

The old frontier was reduced to whitewashed racist tropes on television, and the need for a new frontier, one that spoke to the science, technology, and industry of the midcentury, became painfully obvious. They found this new frontier not in the familiar plane of the American map, but along a third axis. They found it by looking up. Technology and exceptionalism, epitomized by the space race and cold war, had captured the American imagination and identity. For the first time in human history, men were able to reach the heavens, and those men were Americans. This new, super-earthly frontier would be explored with rockets, not wagons.

There was, again, still, a problem. All those roads and cars and gasoline created yet another glut, this time, of petroleum byproducts. But industry had already found a fix for that—plastic. The first entirely synthetic plastic, Bakelite, was invented in New York in 1907. After the surge in innovation driven by the World Wars, there were dozens, hundreds, of new plastic products on the market, and more coming all the time. They were miracles of versatility, easily transmuted for seemingly any purpose with the simple addition of the right ingredients, colorants, fillers, plasticizers, flame retardants, and stabilizers. Chemicals.

In 1935 the DuPont chemicals company adopted the slogan "Better Things for Better Living…Through Chemistry." The goal of the campaign, according to Charles Hackett, the advertising director for the company, was to address the "unspoken fear of bigness in business." Over time, other companies borrowed the phrase, shortening it to "Better Living Through Chemistry" to avoid trademark infringement. Soon, like plastic, it was everywhere. And in some ways, it was true, the American standard of life was extraordinary. Never mind that these wholly new substances, known for their persistence and durability, were leaching some of the very same chemicals they were designed to contain into our bodies, landfills, and waterways. It was a commercial culture shift bigger than just plastic. The mid-twentieth century gave us computers, antibiotics and new vaccines, appliances, motorized and automated agriculture, and so much more. And it was all done under the umbrella of more and better. To keep from reaching consumer capacity, Charles Kettering and GM created "planned obsolescence" and "the organized creation of dissatisfaction." By the mid-1950s, Better Living Through Chemistry and planned obsolescence had morphed the great melting pot's workaday population, from a variegated and dynamic fledgling middle class into the suburban monoculture of the nuclear family.

Americans in the midcentury nuclear family personified a testament to the human race's entry into the Space Race—robust, healthy, and modern. The men were strong and silent in their suits, the women wore corsets and heels for dinner at home, the children, all above average, were spoiled and optimistic. For the (mostly white) families who came to represent the era, it was a time of leisure and accumulation backed by (largely Christian) family values. It had happened quickly, as for the first time there was a truly unified source of media permeating American homes. Their bourgeoisie existence was codified, packaged, and sold to them via television, visual, engrossing, and almost entirely controlled by sponsors and networks. Americans, still in need of solace and escape, embraced all of it turning to visual entertainment, consumption, and, ironically, the American landscape to cure what ailed them.

Perhaps no other single thing represented this strange combination better than the rise of the Western movie genre in the midcentury. Westerns films first became popular during the silent film era, but a churn-and-burn mentality and failure to adapt to the new technology of the talkies hurt them, and, like the rest of the country, cinema in general slumped in 1930s and '40s. But postwar patriotic fervor and nostalgia from the last frontier generation conspired to bring them back, and by the early 1950s, when the nuclear family was most in need of distraction, there were more Western films being released than all the other genres combined.

They relied on a successful formula that was far from the Donna Reed zeitgeist. Most were set in western deserts and those most sacred of American lands, the National Parks—Yosemite, Yellowstone, and the Grand Canyon. In these films, like *High Noon*, *Shane*, and *The Searchers*, Indigenous inhabitants were wrongly depicted as universally unhinged and violent; women as prostitutes or virgin captives; men as gunslingers, drunks, and grifters, and the land as the harshest thing around. Like the tidy plot lines of early family sitcoms, there was always redemption. Personal codes of honor and personal gain took precedence over the rule of law. Freedom was linked to a Christian God; frontier justice was dispatched with impunity. The utopian communism that had been the basis for so much of the occupation of the West was nowhere to be found.

Across America, an entire generation of children born a hundred years after the Applegates migrated west opened the frontier in their imaginations, playing cowboys and Indians in front yards with plastic toys. Toward the end of the decade, several things coalesced, pushing against the narrative of the nuclear norm. The effects of radioactivity on a broad swath of the country, the "down winders," were setting in. People were getting sick in spite of the Atomic Energy Commission's previous assurance of nuclear technology's safety and promotion of test sites as tourist attractions. Other chemicals were starting to cause concern. Rachel Carson warned of a silent spring. The Civil Rights movement gained momentum. Allen Ginsberg rasied the battle cry in his poem "Howl", describing what he called "the best minds" of his generation in the grips of madness. All those entitled baby boomers, just then coming of age, began to question the status quo. They had been raised in a plastic fantastic world and were beginning to realize it. Then, in 1967 Jefferson Airplane released the album *Surrealistic Pillow* with "White Rabbit" and "Plastic Fantastic Lover" as back-to-back tracks, and listed an unknown artist named Jerry Garcia as "spiritual advisor" on the album. They became siren songs for something completely new. Again.

SIGNPOST

Disneyland opened in Anaheim, California, in July 1955. Even on that first day, the road to the entrance was jammed with cars. Inside, the new asphalt was so fresh that women's high-heeled shoes sank into it like primordial muck. There wasn't any water, the drinking fountains were dry, leaving everyone thirsty in scorching summer heat. In time though, as Disney continued to capture American's hearts and imaginations, Disneyland became a mecca of American escapism, the gold standard of western entertainment enterprises. It would become the most visited theme park in the world.

TWELVE

TRAIL STORY: THE BOY WITH THE MOUSE EARS

"But now that it's too late, I know I should never have been in television. I don't know what else I should have done. Maybe grown up with my family like a kid."

—DENNIS DAY, 1971

NOTHING SAYS AMERICA LIKE BUFFALO BILL, EXCEPT MAYBE Mickey Mouse, especially in the mid-twentieth century when Americans were full of patriotic fever and postwar optimism. This, however, is not a story about Mickey. It's a story about a boy who came to be a part of the American Dream. It's a story about a boy whose life was defined by it, who was cherished as an American treasure, and what became of him. This is a story about how we took care of that dream.

Dennis Day was born in Las Vegas in 1942 but moved with his parents and sister to Los Angeles when he was young. Their mother, a fan of Hollywood musicals, had enrolled her children early on in singing and dancing lessons and would regularly sign them up for local talent shows. Dennis and his sister spent a lot of their time practicing in their family's garage. Dennis, blond, big eared, freckled, with an easy, wide grin and flappy ears, had something special and it showed. By age eleven Hollywood noticed, casting him in a small role in the 1953 movie *A Lion Is in the Streets* with James Cagney. A year later Disney called, asking if Dennis wanted to audition for a new variety show they were casting. Did Dennis, they asked, want to be a Mouseketeer?

He did. Of course he did. So, in 1955 Dennis signed on to appear as a Mouseketeer on Disney's *The Mickey Mouse Club* TV show. He was twelve years old.

The show, hosted by Jimmie Dodd and Roy Williams, featured its own revolving cast of singing and dancing kids and teens, including Annette Funicello, Cubby O'Brien, and Doreen Tracey. It was a mix of mini-mystery dramas, Disney animated shorts, comic skits, and lots and lots of singing and dancing, and it aired on ABC weeknights and was rebroadcast weekday afternoons right after *American Bandstand.* The show was supposed to be a vehicle for Disney products, but it was really more of a vehicle for social norms regarding morality, gender, sexuality, and a host of other topics. Most of the songs and many of the shorts included lessons in, and admonitions about, romance and dating wrapped in Americana—western themes like hay rides and mining were ubiquitous. The Mickey Mouse Club, broadcast daily to millions of young people across the country, were to be models of mid-century American values and aesthetics.

To that end, there was a Mouseketeer for every (white) kid. The hallmark of the show was the roll call, in which the Mouseketeers often appeared in their iconic costumes—short-sleeved turtleneck sweaters with their names printed in bold letters high across their chests and, of course, a pair of Mickey Mouse ears—and shouted out their names during a lively song-and-dance number. Only the most popular of the Mouseketeers were showcased in this way, those the production team internally called the "Red Team." Dennis didn't make the Red Team his first year, instead finding himself among the lower-ranking Blue Team. Still, it was a step above the White Team and ensured his presence in almost every show. With hard work, he made it to the Red Team the second year. And he did work hard. His sister recalled in an interview that he was gone from dawn until dusk the entire time he was with the show. He was delighted, and it showed. In one roll call, a grinning Dennis, dressed as a cowboy, emerges triumphantly from a stagecoach to announce his name and gallop an imaginary horse across the stage in front of a façade-western town.

He was charming. Dennis, like all of the Mouseketeers, was hugely talented, able to tap dance as well as he could act. He was just as likely to hop across the stage dressed as an oil rigger on a pogo stick or dance the Charleston as he was to play the banjo on Fun with Music Day. And the audience ate it all up, quickly turning the group into cultural icons and the Mickey Mouse Club into the most-viewed daytime show on television. But he did lack one essential talent—singing—which was ubiquitous on the show. It mattered. As one fan would later write on a Facebook page devoted to memorializing the Club, "Dennis was nobody's favorite Mouseketeer." To stay on the show, you had to be a lot of people's favorite Mouseketeer.

After just two years, he was released from his contract, and in 1957 he left the show.

In 1960, as soon as he had turned eighteen, Dennis came out as gay and moved to San Francisco. He continued to work as an actor, traveling to gigs in Los Angeles and New York. In the Big Apple, he became a part of the burgeoning experimental-theater scene, taking the stage at the infamous Theater La MaMa, which would go on to incubate acts like the Blue Man Group and Bette Midler's early avant-comedy.

By his own admission, and very much in keeping with the times, he dabbled in drugs.

For a while, it seemed like he would make a living, if not a legacy, acting. He produced musicals and happenings throughout the Bay Area and taught community theater workshops and dance. For a while in the late sixties, he lived in Los Angeles, where he ran the county's community theater program. But he never got another big break and always had to supplement his income, usually working odd jobs in retail.

Eventually, he fell in love. Henry Ernest Caswell was twelve years his senior, a UC Berkeley graduate with a master's degree in religious studies, and a priest in the Christ Catholic Church, an eastern orthodox sect of Catholicism. They met at a Renaissance Faire, a kind of early cosplay festival popular on the west coast. At these events, artisans and performers came together in counterculture craft fairs with an old-world twist. It was something that appealed to an alienated generation that read a lot of Tolkien, had taken its fair share of drugs, and would soon drop out to go back to the land. Dennis had immersed himself in the Renaissance Faire scene, becoming something of a luminary in what would eventually evolve into summer arts festivals like Lightning in a Bottle and Burning Man. It fit with his value system and sense of spirit. The Renaissance Faires all had an environmental ethic and were located in beautiful places. The land was considered as magical as the fairs themselves, and often the community sought to protect and preserve those sites.

There was an age difference, but it didn't seem to matter; the two got on well and for some time they lived in the Bay

Area together, where they ran a guest house for gay actors. Dennis worked for the Living History Centre, helping to produce Renaissance and Dickens Christmas fairs. They were happy. "Dennis would call and tell my mom, tell her he met this wonderful man," his sister would later tell *Dateline* about Dennis's early relationship with Ernie. "Ernie started coming to Christmas every year. He was a part of our family."

But the *Mickey Mouse Club* never really went away. The boomers who tuned in, turned on, and dropped out hadn't forgotten Dennis's wide grin, and he was recognized often. In 1968, with most of the boomers and Mouseketeers now solidly in their twenties and starting to have their own children, Disney thought it was a good time to infuse its fans with some nostalgia. Would Dennis, they asked, like to do a reunion show?

Of course he did. Well, sort of.

In an interview with *Rolling Stone* three years later, Dennis recalled the experience as fraught at best, filled with the same rushed and dictatorial energy that dominated many of his memories from the original show. It was obvious to him that he no longer fit the Disney role, and it triggered doubts if he ever had. That show, he recalled, was the hardest he had ever had to work to craft a smile wide enough to satisfy the producers. He went home from rehearsals for the reunion as he had often as a young Mouseketeer, his face aching from the effort.

By the time Disney called in 1980 about a second reunion, the romance was clearly over. Dennis appeared but was slighted, one of only two Red Team members to be left out of the primary cast. Instead, he was relegated to the Blue Team, appearing only as a backup singer and dancer in the beginning and ending acts. In the finale, he can be seen at the far end of the back row, standing slightly apart from his fellow performers as they sing their trademark goodbye— "M-I-C (See you soon!) K-E-Y (Why? Because we like you!) M-O-U-S-Eeee!"

Shortly after the reunion, Dennis and Ernie packed up and moved to a town called Ashland in southern Oregon. Ashland had been the home of the Oregon Shakespeare Festival since 1935 and by the 1980s the event had turned a corner in popularity. It ran from February to October each year and drew tens of thousands of Shakespeare and Renaissance fans. The festival so completely dominated the city's culture that its downtown core was modeled to look like an Elizabethan hamlet. The 1970s had brought an influx of liberalism to the tiny college town along with members of the radical faerie movement. The radical faeries were people, mostly men, who believed that broad-based, environmentally minded, largely secular spirituality could, and should be, an essential component of modern queerness. It was a movement based on radical acceptance, self-expression, and joy.

Dennis and Ernie thought they had found heaven.

They dove into the festival community and for years continued to make pilgrimages south to their Faire families in California. Eventually though, opportunities for aging actors became more and more scarce, and money got tight. And as the popularity of the festival exploded in the 1990s, more and more Californians purchased houses in the area, sending the cost of living through the roof. The couple was forced north eight miles up the Applegate Trail to Phoenix, where they bought a modest single-story brick house on a narrow street with no sidewalks that abutted the town's old pioneer cemetery.

There, they made a quiet life. Dennis had a long-standing interest in Dickensian-era treats—he had even written an illustrated Dickensian Christmas cookbook. The two began a small business making wine, jams and jellies, and confections to sell at Faires and local markets, Creature Comfits. To supplement their income, Dennis worked at Harry & David, a holiday fruit gift basket company whose headquarters were in nearby Medford, a hangover from the region's boom and bust fruit production days. Eventually Dennis's time as a Mouseketeer faded like the rest of the Applegate Trail.

THIRTEEN

TUNED IN, TURNED ON, DROPPED OUT, 1968–1980

THE WORLD YOU THINK YOU INHABIT, THE ONE SHOWN SO tangibly and reliably on the map, doesn't really exist. It's a fantasy, a story that we tell ourselves, a reflection of what we think we know and, at base, a projection of our own ideas and beliefs and institutions. It's an image of reality, based on measured truths but like light passed through a prism, it's distorted and refracted. *It's, like, just what someone wants you to believe, man.*

The world being round has always presented a problem for wayfaring travelers in need of a means of navigation aids suitable for transport. Globes become cumbersome quickly and do not lend themselves to scaling. Maps, with their inherit lightness, high resolution, and ability to be rolled and folded and tucked away, are far more suitable. But translating the material so accurately captured on a globe onto the two-dimensional surface of a map isn't a straightforward process. Globes peel rather than unroll, and in the flattening, great wedges of open space, space that doesn't exist in reality, are created between the strips. Cartographers attempt to resolve this problem by bending the edges of the map or filling in those blanks with extra bits of ocean or land. The hows and whys of what gets distorted are due to another kind of projection altogether, map projection.

Map projections are the result of a process by which three-dimensional relationships are translated into two-dimensional spaces by passing lines through intersection points with a plane, like light passes through film. Choices are involved. Different map projections are the result of different choices. There is always a compromise. Something is always distorted, landforms stretched too long, too squat, or altogether far too large. The effect is most pronounced in world maps, and on those, most often toward the poles. When most of us picture a map of the world, we picture it in Mercator projection.

Mercator, which uses the concept of cylindrical projection, was invented by the Flemish cartographer and geographer Gerardus Mercator in 1569. It was easy to read and accurately depicted the major trade routes and population centers of the western world. And for the next three hundred years, no one really questioned it. That it made Greenland appear to be its own continent roughly the size of North America when that was plainly untrue didn't seem to bother anyone. That the world we saw on globes could be so substantially different from that depicted on the map became a background-level cognitive dissonance. *You're just seeing what The Man wants you to see, man. You gotta wake up and see the world for what it really is, a broken, slivered place.*

Then something interesting happened. Right around the same time that the CIA started experimenting with mind control and perception-altering drugs in the mid-twentieth century, there was a revolution of sorts in the cartographic world. Mapmakers and users pushed for the introduction of new kinds of projections that called into question distortions that had come to be taken for granted; these new projections began to reshape the average person's worldview. The results, which upended people's concepts of distance, relative size, and centrality, were challenging to accept.

American society in the 1960s suffered a similar kind of splintering distortion and cognitive dissonance when issues of race, class, gender, and sexuality collided with a new and unexpected product of midcentury better living through chemistry—the consciousness-altering effects of psychedelics. The CIA had created a new synthesized drug they hoped would let them control the minds of their sometimes-unwitting test subjects as part of the MKUltra program. You know it as LSD and its main purpose was to create complicity. Better control through chemistry.

It was a project that backfired, most notably due to the efforts of Ken Kesey, an all-American wrestler turned writer raised along the northern reaches of the Applegate Trail who had stumbled into a seemingly benign medical experiment only to find himself in possession of a mind-altering substance that tested and expanded the limits of one's consciousness. It didn't take very long for him to steal some of the new drug and share it with the burgeoning hippie counterculture scene of the Bay Area, where he attended Stanford's illustrious writing program. He started hosting happenings termed Acid Tests, triptastic parties rigged to blow the minds of the newly initiated. With the help of the Hells Angels' distribution network and the guru-like following that was forming around his house band, the Grateful Dead, the Acid Tests became the lynchpin of the mind-expanding counterculture movement.

Kesey capitalized on and expanded his new following by providing the entire generation of postwar young Americans a disquisition on reality, his best-selling novel, *One Flew Over the*

Cuckoo's Nest. In it, Kesey casts a mental institution ward as a microcosm of the United States, and the inmates as heroes resisting its tyranny. The novel's message of anti-institutionalism and free thinking resonated with the first American generation to be raised by televisions, the children of the postwar boom for whom everything had been so neatly packaged into consumer goods. When the established academic elite, like Harvard professors, doctors Timothy Leary and Richard Alpert (Ram Dass), joined in with musicians, writers, and other artists advocating mind expansion via substance use (and a number of other alternative ways of being) as a means to break free of the mental confines of midcentury life, American boomers listened. Soon it seemed everyone was getting on the proverbial bus, heading toward yet another frontier that seemed to hover just out of reach, like a mirage on the western horizon.

LSD did more than just lead these new pioneers into a party. It forced them to question reality. Many didn't like what they saw: Social injustice, war mongering, class inequality, and the impacts of capitalism and all that better living through chemistry had on the environment became outsized like Greenland in their new projection. But how to resist? For that, they turned again to Leary, who had by then boiled the results of this new consciousness down to a single catch phrase: Tune In, Turn On, Drop Out.

What seemed like moments later, the boomers, just coming of age, did just that. Seemingly all at once they collectively decided to cast off their Mickey Mouse ears, free themselves of the physical and mental confines of the time, and enter the age of Aquarius. They left home in droves, forsaking normative ways of living, family structures, sexual mores, racist civil structures, and consumerism to get "on the bus." For the vast majority of these pilgrims, that bus, literally and figuratively, was heading west. The movement reached its mainstream apex in the summer of 1968, just as the United States declared a de facto abandonment of the gold standard.

The zeitgeist was changing in ways far larger than drugs and popular music. People's minds were being opened to all kinds of new realities and ways of thinking, especially with respect to better living through chemistry. Soon, DDT, the effects of leaded paint and gasoline, and later, the horrors of Love Canal would all demonstrate the power of chemicals to decimate ecosystems and ravage human bodies. Perhaps the best example of this new way of thinking was the Wilderness Act of 1964, which set aside areas of exceptional inherent value to be left untouched by humans, and in doing so codified the term "wilderness." The moment was termed "the greening of America" by Charles Reich in his 1970 best seller of the same name, a rebellion against the accepted mainstream, most notably industrialization or "a robot life, in which man is deprived of his own being, and he becomes instead a mere role, occupation, or function." Reich and his contemporaries, even Kesey and his pranksters, agreed in broad concept that there was a pressing need to cultivate a new consciousness, one rooted in personal liberties and truth to oneself as well as to the natural world. Of wilderness, Edward Abbey, a hero of the generation said in his 1968 best seller *Desert Solitaire: A Season in the Wilderness*, "Wilderness is not a luxury but a necessity of the human spirit, and as vital to our lives as water and good bread," .

On this, it seemed most everyone agreed. Everyone in America to some degree had returned to the wild. For the conservative mainstream, it was through family vacations to National Parks, hunting parties, and water skiing on newly constructed reservoirs;

and for the radical left, it was through communes, be-ins, and outdoor summer festivals and medieval fairs. It seemed everyone saw some reason to return to the garden, but none more than the Back to the Landers.

Disillusioned by the institutional response to the civil rights movement, the struggle for women's rights, the ongoing conflict in Vietnam, and threat of nuclear war, many, many young people took dropping out literally, settling on rural land in intentional communities, cooperatives, communes, and chosen family units. Across the country, tens of thousands of people, dubbed by Fred Turner as the "New Communalists," abandoned the urban centers and suburbs of their youth to go "back to the land." Contrary to much of the dopehead-dropout sentiment mainstream media attached to them, it wasn't just about following Kesey and the Grateful Dead.

The Back to the Land and new communalism movements represented tangible manifestations of the shift in mainstream consciousness, as participants, mostly members of the largest generation America had ever seen, the boomers, attempted to rewrite the American relationship to each other and to the environment. Many of them settled in the privacy of Oregon's secluded, arable valleys along the forgotten Applegate Trail, where land and a good life were still cheap. More than that, Oregon Country still had an air of lawless, unimpeded liberty that appealed to people looking to reinvent themselves and their ways of living. Once there, they adopted a pseudo-agrarian way of life based on the midcentury ideals of freedom, subsistence, and rugged individualism they had been raised on. It was spurred by the mind-expansion of the 1960s and the war in Vietnam and the civil rights movements, sure, but it was also tied up in the paired realities of an economy that was finally beginning to wane, and the toll the that drugs and excess was beginning to take on their bodies. They held in common a determination to forge a new, counter–consumer culture way of life rooted in subsistence and Marx-inspired communism.

Writer Gary Snyder, an outdoor enthusiast and mountain climber from Oregon who is largely credited with the popularization of Zen Buddhist principles in the West, captured the generational view of the time when he wrote: "Forest equals crop/ Scenery equals recreation/Public equals money/The shopkeeper's view of Nature." In doing so he encapsulated the history of the American relationship to the land in the United States. Like Snyder, Back to the Landers and communers were overwhelmingly idealists, deeply spiritual, and largely ecumenical. Under Snyder's influence and that of newly Westernized guruism, they blended aspects of Asian and what they perceived to be Native American cultural and spiritual practices with evangelical and orthodox Christian practices and, by all accounts, large amounts of drugs. What resulted was a slew of new philosophies, religions, and even cults. Jesus People, the Shilohs, New Ageism, Hare Krishnas, and Westernized Taoism all exploded, as did participation in the Radical Faerie movement, Wicca, neo-paganism, and Gaianism.

The combination of these new ideologies with the realities of dropping out and going back to the land had its own, more practical consequence. Quickly after taking up their hoes, idealistic boomers discovered the need for a new skill set, one that would boost the yields of their organic gardens, lower their electricity bills, and reduce their water use. Necessity became the mother of invention and they began to call for and devise new "appropriate technologies," alternative fuels and power sources, and low-impact, sustainable farming practices like permaculture and bioregionalism. A new branch of feminist thought, ecofeminism, emerged, which deconstructed the masculinized, colonial notions of the environment and wildness/wilderness that had, and still does, dominated so much of American history. Fundamental to ecofeminism was the recognition that the oppression of the natural world cannot be separated from the oppression of humans, particularly women. In doing so, ecofeminists helped lay the groundwork for postmillennial intersectional feminism.

Ecology, that most Humboldtian of sciences, made a surprising comeback during this period, applied to a secular philosophy that dominated environmental studies through the end of the twentieth century—deep ecology. Deep ecology was unique and influential because it bridged the gap between the investigation-driven sciences of the twentieth century and the new consciousness of the boomer generation. Unlike other branches of science, deep ecology sought to connect the human spirit to our understanding of the natural world. It also recognized the importance of diversity in natural systems, the rights of people to fulfill their vital needs, the negative impacts of humanity and its population growth, policies, and behaviors, the dangers of growth-based standards of living, and the obligation for individuals to take substantive action in the face of those truths. In so doing, it required of its practitioners what they termed an indulgence of the soul—joy. To take action, deep ecologists argued, one must have hope.

Incredibly, many of these ideas made their way into the mainstream, a product, perhaps, of the sheer number of boomers who had passed the acid tests. It seemed that the concept of environmental posterity had finally reached American consciousness, and its prospects did not look good. The ideas of communes, cooperatives, and community movements shifted from rural communities to cities where people formed businesses using cooperative models, rallied for the creation of parks and green spaces, clean water, fresh air, and community gardens, and won battles in favor of civil rights and against the war in Vietnam. Kesey's books were made into Academy Award–winning movies, and previously fringe products like natural yogurt and tofu became widely available. Yoga, multiculturalism, and educational television broke into the mainstream, as did the pill and the right to an abortion. Americans changed. For the first time in the twentieth century, Americans had begun to internalize and process the distant consequences of consumption and chemicals.

In truth, it wasn't entirely by choice. Though the benefits of the cultural revolution were tangible amid human society, it faltered when applied to the American relationship to the environment. The harsh reality was that they were starting to run out of land, trees to build new houses, tracts to put them on, and clean water to pump through pipes. And it was crowded. Dumps filled to overflowing, sewage systems needed to be upgraded, and toxic smog lingered over cities. Americans were forced to consider the possibility that the land and its resources were finite, and that their treatment of it tantamount to suicide.

The government changed, too. Nixon, though a crook, proved to be a dependably environmentally minded president. That he was a Quaker may have influenced him to some degree, but his environmental policy was almost certainly more driven by his desire to expand his voter base. The first Earth Day was held in 1970, and it garnered the celebration's largest turnout, an estimated 20 million people at tens of thousands of locations, for a politically motivated event, the first of its kind in the nation. Its message was clear: Americans valued the environment and were willing to take action to protect it.

The Environmental Protection Agency was established by the end of the year, and the decade to come would bring protective legislation including the Endangered Species and Clean Water acts. Congress also expanded the role of the Forest Service to include ecosystem management such as fishing and hunting regulation and recreation services in addition to forestry and logging. In doing so, it aligned itself with some of the values of deep ecology, recognizing that there was more to be gained from forests than just trees or revenue, and that public lands could and should be used to impact the overall health of the environment and that of people, now and into the future. Nixon's government didn't stop there; it even went so far as to contract with a "hippie for hire" cooperative, founded in the timberlands of Oregon's Applegate country, to run the opposing arm to its logging operations—replanting. The Hoedads Reforestation Cooperative, worker owned and operated, broke all kinds of rules and taboos left over from the days of the Wild West, including the males-only rule of forestry work. Importantly, they were some of the first timber-industry insiders to raise alarms over the effects of herbicides and pesticides, often recording the toxic impacts in their own broken and sickened bodies. They quickly became the national model for the workers-cooperative movement, employing thousands of workers across the country.

Ultimately, though, the revolution? It fell apart, even the Hoedads, whose seemingly iron-clad relationship with big timber made it look impervious to destructive forces. Nothing is ever simple. There were a lot of reasons. New religious groups didn't have the cultural and traditional underpinnings of more established practices and therefore tended to fade as their participants aged. Communes, tasked with re-creating nearly every aspect of life, often while attempting to achieve group consensus, tended to adopt internalized patterns, especially in terms of gender roles and division of labor. White men were commonly in charge, helped by issues of redlining, lack of credit availability to women, and other institutional privileges that lent themselves to white male dominance even in these radical communities. De facto racial segregation was pervasive, and as children were born, more traditional family structures began to emerge, pushing people out of cooperative and communal structures.

And as for policy? Inroads to policy changes had been made, though they were still held well in check by industry. Even the idea of cooperatives as a legal concept came under attack from government, local and federal, who sought to close what they viewed as loopholes in tax and wage structures of the groups. There were other issues, too, concerning finances, the challenges of navigating communal culture, drug use and abuse, and new sexual mores. Within a decade, this boomer-driven, second-wave communism had largely collapsed, and a new era of environmental backlash and anti-environmentalism, driven by Ronald Regan's administration, took over. Americans forsook the land and sequestered in shopping malls. Casual wanna-be Yippies became hard-core yuppies, and the baby boomers moved back to the suburbs, this time to stay. The effects of the transition period were recorded in the forests along the Applegate Trail, whose trees were logged at rates equal to and greater than the deforestation of the Amazon rainforests. By the late 1970s, half of Oregon's timber came from public land. Ultimately, it was just *hard*. "By the end of the season people can do without each other for a good, long time." said one Hoedad in their quarterly newsletter in 1978.

Maybe all that idealism and contrariness had just run that same predictable course carved out by gold miners and missionaries a hundred years earlier.

Kesey certainly seemed to think so. In 1971 the movie *Sometimes a Great Notion*, based on his book of the same name, came out starring Henry Fonda, a mainstay of the flagging Western-film genre. It told the story of a logging family through the stereotypical male lens of western machismo, their struggles to keep their small "gyppo" operation afloat in the midst of changing times and against a tidal river that threatens to wash away their homestead. *Gyppo* is a term unique to Oregon Country that denotes someone who runs or works for a small-scale logging operation outside of established, large-scale sawmills and lumber companies. It was coined at the beginning of World War I by a cooperative, the Industrial Workers of the World, who saw these independent businesses as strike breakers. By Kesey's time, however, they were viewed as heroes of independence from corporate giants, not scabs. It is a story of exhausted resources and eroded dreams that leaves little hope for the future. The title refers to the old blues tune "Goodnight, Irene":

Sometimes I lives in the country
Sometimes I lives in the town
Sometimes I haves a great notion
To jump into the river an' drown

In the years after the first Earth Day, LSD turned into white drugs, and the scene got heavy. When the hippies looked around for Ken Kesey and his Merry Pranksters, who had been forever memorialized by Tom Wolfe's *The Electric Kool-Aid Acid Test* (the same author who cemented the Space Race in American history with *The Right Stuff*), they couldn't find them. Kesey and company had packed it up and headed out of California and back up north, to Oregon Country, intent on forging an alternative lifestyle along the Applegate Trail in an old farmhouse on a piece of property they called the Promised Land.

And what of all those newfangled map projections that promised to bring greater clarity and understanding of our world? The Mercator map projection continued to be widely used, but inroads had been made. In atlases and textbooks, the Mercator projection slowly began to be replaced by more accurate projections that aimed to address those issues of truth and distortion that had so long been relied upon. The map that was once so empty seemed suddenly filled with people and places and stuff. This time, the lines that cut across it were not rails, but freeways and flight lines. The only emptiness left to the west was the sea.

SIGNPOST

In 1969, inspired by the Renaissance Faires in California, a group of communes and Back to the Landers held a similar event in a city park in Eugene, Oregon. After several iterations, the event regrouped as an arts and music festival and took up residence on a plot of oak forest and open grassland thirty miles outside the city on a western branch of the Applegate Trail. Over time, it would become one of the region's iconic events, The Oregon Country Fair. But in the early 1970s, it was considered little more than just a hippie party in a vacant grassy field. No one knew that it would soon inspire the entirety of neo-tribal festival culture, culminating in Burning Man, which would take up residence some twenty years later in the Black Rock desert, just miles from the Humboldt Sink on the far end of the Applegate Trail. In the earliest years of the event, Ken Kesey and his Merry Pranksters coaxed the Grateful Dead to play a benefit concert for his brother's failing Creamery business. They called it The Field Trip.

FOURTEEN

TRAIL STORY: THE FIELD TRIP

OLD RENAISSANCE FAIRGROUNDS, VENETA, OREGON, AUGUST 27, 1972

THE TRAFFIC JAM WAS EPIC AND NOBODY CARED. WINDOWS down, radios playing, pumping out James Brown, Zappa, Steely Dan. All along the rural highway vans were parked, some broken down, some just chilling out, hitching rides. Everyone headed to the same place, just following the yellow lines of the road, a caravan of hippies and Jesus freaks making their way out to a dusty meadow in a town nobody ever heard of.

They arrived in waves—first the locals, mostly the "in crowd" that satellited around Kesey and his Pranksters, and the Tribes, the communes and collectives that used the property for their twice-yearly Renaissance Faire. That happened in the woods, but not this, this was in the open field, the parking area, with not a tree in sight. Nothing but the stage and Owsley's massive sound system that took forever to set up. Anyways, it was hot right away, first thing in the morning, and everybody was in a hurry, guys still putting up the stage and Kesey's there with the bus and Owsley's right of out prison. There's all these cats running around, the Rainbow people and White Bird, and the Hog Farm and the Hoedads. Who was in charge of this thing? Kesey? The Dead? Was there even security? How the hell did they think they were going to pull this off?

It's hot and everything is sunburned, especially the skinny, wide-grinned hippies working security and directing traffic, or at least standing in strategic places and waving and smiling as the cars bumped and rolled across the field, wheels spinning on the too-hot grass. Scattered along the improvised trail, freaks and far-outs make their way from their cars to the stage, hauling blankets and food and nothing at all.

And all because Kesey's brother was in a jam. Everybody's in a jam these days. Fucking Nixon....

I swear to God the tickets are printed on the back of yogurt labels or something. Is this some kind of benefit concert? Yeah, man, it's a benefit for freaks. See? Free food over there, and free hugs that way, it's like *give a freak, take a freak....*

And then a microphone goes live and the guys pick up their instruments and Babbs is up there doing his best impersonation of Neal Cassidy doing his best impression of Buster Keaton, which was how Babbs always liked to describe him.

"I hate to say, this is a personal problem here...but we've got evicted from our house in the middle of our walnut grove, so this is the end of any of the walnuts that we'll ever have again from Maple Isle and I'd like to present this to uh, Phil Lesh, the bass player here." Healthy. Homegrown. Walnuts. The drum rolls in, but Babbs keeps talking until his voice fades into noise.

"Over here on the piano is a newer addition to the Grateful Dead..." Bam bam bam! The drums again. They're just making noise now, like they're getting used to how the instruments feel in their hands. Jerry peers out into the sun, his face still round and young under his beard. Black mop of hair. Black T-shirt. Jeans.

"Ok, right on, the Grateful Dead!" Babbs calls into the mic.

And in rolls the band, tight, together, fast-jamming, and on key, to Chuck Berry's "Promised Land." And people are lounging on their blankets and the white sunshade across the stage flaps like a flag and everybody's going down with the undertow, out to Kesey's Promised Land.

You know Kesey lives over on the Promised Land, that's what he says, over at the base of Mount Pisgah. That's in the bible man, Pisgah's in the Bible. I thought they said it was by Springfield, by the creamery. Maybe *that's* what these tickets are about about... *is this show a benefit for a fucking yogurt factory?*

Yeah, it's like a family thing. Kesey and the Dead, man, they can't let a poor guy down.

Two songs in, the music starts to drag and roll; they announce it's so hot that their instruments are already out of tune. Chuck and Sue are there with the creamery folks handing out yogurt as fast as they can. There's cameras everywhere, like proper film cameras, because it's Kesey and Kesey records everything he ever does, and on the radio people are freaking out about the heat.

"We've gotta get some water to these people."

The Dead, the Pranksters, they considered it as all-American as it could get, just freedom and individuals and a whole bunch of right-on people exploring a whole new territory. Because that's what Americans did. Explore new territory. And they were all there trying to make America a better place. A groovier place, a place where people treated each other better.

The free yogurt didn't last very long and there was never any water.

Augustus Owsley "Bear" Stanley III. "Owsley". Already a legend. Not in the Oxford dictionary yet, but he and his LSD would be, eventually. Delirium sets in and now people are streaming in from all directions, walking through the woods with coolers, tube socks still white. Some came in down the Long Tom River, but mostly they streamed through the makeshift ticket gates, then over and around them, tickets, few, catching the wind like that white sunshade flying over Jerry's head. This thing is free, right? Everything's free. But it's a benefit? Steal this concert and your face.

What's wrong with my face?

All the water's dosed. Everything is dosed. It's a Kesey thing, man. This is the *field trip*. The last acid test. The heat wouldn't stop them from dosing the water. But man, the way the sun beat down on that stretch of grass, the way the dust stuck to the humid air.

Then Babbs, fucking Babbs, right? He's up onstage introducing the band…or did that already happen?

How did we get here? What's the point of this thing? Is there a point to all this? There's gotta be a point because this thing is *happening*.

We came down that road. Which road? *The* road. Forget it. You're here, we're all fucking here and *that's* what it's all about. It's about a new way of life, man, like organic food and chilling out, and being able to smoke pot and fuck and do whatever and not having to be so fucking uptight and unhappy anymore. Not being taken down when the wagon comes, you know? Just, shaking it all off, the whole, fucking nightmare, just shaking it off.

I've never seen so many nipples in my entire life. Well, it's hot. What the fuck does that have to do with it? I'm just saying

I've never seen so many naked people in one place before in my entire life. I've never seen this many naked people at all. I mean, that guy's got nothing but a flute in his hand.

"We've gotta get some water into these people, man...."

The people don't care. They dance. Bare-bottomed, arms flailing, knees lifting in a kind of ecstatic crane-dance. Others are just running around the farther reaches of the field naked, their faces the same color as their beet-red bottoms, a melted, ecstatic, moving, tripped-out mass some 20,000 strong. Out of nowhere some dude parachutes into the crowd and hardly anybody notices because the jam goes on.

"Just hang in, we're gonna move with the truck just so you know what you're getting hit with. So nobody thinks it's something weird coming down on them...it's just water...from the crick."

Every few songs they make another announcement about lost children and water. "Jack Straw" is playing, and look, there's one of them now, dirty faced and sitting in an old tire slurping away at an ice cream cone. Where the hell does a toddler get an ice cream cone in this scene?

Kesey's up there again, or maybe Babbs, or I'm not even sure since they keep calling themselves Poppinjay the Deejay and Brother Bartholomew, but whichever one it is, the other one is wearing this straw cowboy hat and a kind of light blue cowboy shirt like he's going to a Dolly Parton show and *"popping deejay all the way."*

By "Sugar Magnolia" the whole thing's pretty twisted. The band's frenetic pace is wearing people out and the heat is starting to turn things sideways, but that doesn't slow down the jam, and these Oregon hippies prove they have some grit, or something, that gets them through another Saturday night.

At some point half the crowd joins hands and rises up from the ground, arms lifted high as the drums roll out, and it's like they're connected by an invisible thread, and they become a collective, not a sea of individuals but a commonality that extends beyond the music. And they're proving the reason that we all came here, right? Isn't this really what it's all about? Family and community and just playing Frisbee naked in a field because we can and nobody cares?

Jesus, man, have you looked at this place? It's fucking paradise. Look at the size of those fucking trees. What do you call those trees? And there's so much land, we can live here in the forest and use composting toilets and eat organic food and be free, man. We can be like this every day. It's fucking awesome.

Where *did* all these people come from? Everybody's so high it's like they're six feet off the ground—higher because everybody else is so high. And it's a beautiful thing, man, in the face of this uptight culture we're living in. It's another dimension, a parallel universe. I could do this forever.

And then it does go on forever. "Dark Star" spins on for thirty minutes, long enough for people to lose track of where they are, in the song, the set, *hell the whole fucking world, man*. And it's like the only thing still moving is the music and Jerry's fingers over the strings, and he's staring out into the massive crowd and no one's moving anymore except in a slow, uneven sway because nothing exists anymore and the long road that brought them here is empty. And suddenly the sun has gone down or maybe all that rock and roll has reached up and pulled that shining sun down to Planet Earth.

FIFTEEN

SAVE THE ______, 1980–2000

"We the People of the United States, in Order to form a more perfect Union, establish Justice, ensure domestic Tranquility, provide for the common defense, promote the general Welfare, and secure the Blessings of Liberty to ourselves and our Posterity, do ordain and establish this Constitution for the United States of America."

—U.S. CONSTITUTION, 1787

THE THING ABOUT POSTERITY IS, IT REALLY ONLY EVER EXISTS in the abstract. From a place of comfort and security such as the viewpoint afforded the midcentury generation raised in wealth and abundance, posterity is little more than a mirage. For such a generation, posterity may even somehow be more connected to the current moment's legacy than the well-being of the distant future's population or even that of their own children. If the largess of the United Sates in the twentieth century, literal and figurative, did anything, it allowed postwar Americans to live wantonly, secure in their belief in future prosperity and abundance. This was particularly true in terms of the environment. According to Ernest Partridge in *A Companion to Environmental Philosophy*, before the first Earth Day, April 22, 1970, the Philosopher's Index, a compendium of philosophical terms and research dating back to 1902, listed less than ten entries under posterity. The future, until that time, had been wide open.

The economic troubles of the 1970s did not dampen this outlook. Rather, the idealism of the 1970s Back to the Land and communal movements in many ways was driven by it. The hippie's desire for sustainability, renewable energy, and appropriate transportation were all rooted in the beginnings of the recognition that humanity's abundance in the future may not be secure, and that people may have something to do with that. To what degree the current population was responsible to future generations, or to what extent those future generations may have rights, was still uncertain.

Environmentalists at the end of the twentieth century lacked no such clarity.

Traditional conservation groups like the Sierra Club and the Audubon Society had continued to dominate the environmental movement into the last quarter of the century. But theirs were movements built on the ideals of the late 1800s, not the uncertainties of the New Age. Central to their conservation work were bygone assumptions of access, benign use, and management by "humans," a term that in the outdoor industry still largely referred to "white men." Also central to the viewpoint of these groups were midcentury ideas concerning the inherent necessity and benefits of consumption and resource management. By the 1980s, such groups had also shown a willingness to work from within the established economic and political system, one that had been rigged to favor corporate interests from the start.

In doing so, these groups, including the Sierra Club, compromised. Often. One of the most controversial forms of compromise was a practice known as site swapping. In one such instance in the 1950s, the Sierra Club led a campaign aimed at blocking the construction of a dam on the Green River that would have submerged portions of Dinosaur National Monument in Utah. To win the battle against the Federal Bureau of Reclamation and the Bechtel Corporation, they compromised. They would not object to a similar project in Glen Canyon, Arizona if the Green River project was stopped. It worked, sort of. They saved Dinosaur Monument but the Glen Canyon Dam project also allowed one of the largest coal mines in the world to be placed on Navajo land. A decade later, in 1966, the group endorsed the construction of the Diablo Canyon nuclear power plant in an effort to preserve the Nipomo Dunes in California, which was thought to be the more extraordinary natural site of the two. That decision created a controversy that, according to the *San Francisco Chronicle* at the time, "delighted" the Pacific Gas & Electric Company and ultimately resulted in a break in the Sierra Club's ranks and the formation of the group the Friends of the Earth. Despite years of member and public outcry, the board voted against opposing nuclear power facilities at least three more times before finally establishing an anti-nuclear policy in 1974, holding to its support of the Diablo Canyon project until 1979 when the accident at Three Mile Island finally tipped the balance of opinion.

While these battles were taking place, the national population continued to grow, surpassing 226,000,000 in 1980. Industry, especially the manufacturing of cars, which had reached an apex in the mid-1970s, began to decline. A hundred years of encroachment, consumption, chemistry, and compromise converged. Interest rates rose to nearly twenty percent, and inflation climbed into the double digits. The myth of American abundance began to fail and along with it, things like salmon runs and human health. A former anti-communist FBI informer and born-again actor with mediocre grades was elected president in a landslide victory. The Gipper and Nancy Reagan occupied the White House and shortly thereafter gifted Americans an escalation of the Cold War and nuclear proliferation, trickle-down economics, deregulation of corporations, and the war on drugs. And all along the Applegate Trail, trees continued to fall at faster and faster rates.

Then four men stood in front of a bulldozer in the Kalmiopsis wilderness, and that was the end of the age of compromise for the environmental movement.

In the beginning, they called it monkey-wrenching. Equipment was sabotaged, trees were spiked, roads were blocked, survey stakes were pulled. Monkey-wrenching. The term was borrowed from Abbey's 1975 novel *The Monkey Wrench Gang* and amplified by his ubiquitous presence at early gatherings of the new environmental movement. It was a controversial practice that placed not only its practitioners in danger, but also loggers and operators, work-a-day guys with families at home who were just trying to make a living. The interruptions to the supply chain and the loss of revenue enraged corporations and government officials alike. But to the newly emerging radical movement, influenced as it was by deep ecology, such measures were not only morally justified, they were morally required.

Then came the kids of Generation X.

They were the *Sesame Street* multicultural generation of the late 1970s and '80s, the offspring of all those idealistic boomers, the children of the far-outs, the woo-woos, and the Back to the Landers, a lot of whom, by that time, had become mainstream. These kids hadn't just drunk the Kool-Aid, they were raised on it. Born between 1965 and 1980, Generation X totaled about two-thirds of their parents' generation in number and therefore weren't considered a substantive target audience for media and manufacturers. They were the first American generation to be raised by divorced parents and were often left to their own devices after school as latchkey kids. This benign neglect was later reflected in their apathy toward mainstream products and music and spurred an ironic attitude toward even the most basic tenets of American life, like pension plans and home ownership.

They were also the first true digital generation. By the time they were walking and talking, computers had arrived to daily life and were integrated into their classrooms. There, they peered into Apple IIes, solving digitally generated spelling and multiplication problems. For many their first real introduction to computers was in the form of the Oregon Trail Game.

The Oregon Trail Game was released in 1985 for that ubiquitous Apple IIe. The goal was to survive the overland crossing of a pixelated western landscape across the Oregon Trail rendered in what would become an iconic shade of electric green. In it, you begin as banker, carpenter, or farmer, departing from Missouri in 1848, at the leading edge of the gold rush. You're given grubstake to prepare ($800 as a carpenter) and told you don't need to spend it all at once. Oxen, clothing, food, ammunition, and a wagon are all things you're told to buy, and you're asked to do the math to figure out what you can afford. Like the real Oregon Trail experience, there are a lot of grifters and a lot of ways to lose. "Each yoke has two oxen, I recommend three yokes at $40 a yoke, how many yoke do you want to buy?" Right there nearly twenty-five percent of your budget is gone to oxen. You learn quickly that's there's no such thing as too much ammunition or too much food. Indigenous people and buffalo served commercial purposes at best (trading and provisions). Children seldom survived, succumbing to illness nearly as often as river crossings. Prostitutes, polio-infected blankets, and cannibalism were conspicuously left out of the narrative. Most of the time you died, usually due to unfair or unexpected circumstances that lent the game a gotcha! feeling while reinforcing the randomness of suffering and the futility of pioneerism specifically, and life, in general. It was not the only existential lesson doled out to this already jaded generation.

Gen X was also the first generation to be taught about something called the greenhouse effect. It was, they were told, caused by all the gasoline used to run all those cars and the coal being used to heat all those houses. If it proceeded as predicted, they were warned, it would spell certain death for most of the species of the world, probably starting with the polar bears. And in Australia, there was a hole in the ozone layer being created by the chemicals in consumer products like the hairspray holding up their sky-high bangs. The ozone layer was, it turned out, was the only thing protecting us from the sun's searing, life-ending radiation. It was possible, they were told, that these problems could result in the drowning of continents, the desertification of the world, and skin cancer for everyone. Venice would sink into the sea. The world would become a dust bowl. Water wars would rage across the continents. And it was also possible, if not likely, that the consequences of these things could unfold in their lifetime, especially if humanity did not take substantive action to protect and preserve the quality and resources of the environment. Also, the whales, and probably thousands of other species, were being hunted and dehabitated into extinction at alarming rates. It seemed logical that humans might be next.

To many young Gen Xers, it all seemed problematic and troubling.

Bill McKibben named this core trouble of the time when he published his book *The End of Nature* in 1989. In it, McKibben stressed that people had always turned to nature as proof of God, either symbolically or by actual manifestation of the divine, but that the tendency begged a central question: If God was, in fact, manifesting in some way in nature, especially in the ways conceptualized by the American Judeo-Christian tradition, "Why doesn't God stop us from destroying the planet and ourselves along with it?" The answer was a disheartening take on the diametric opposition of science and religion and the choice that humanity had made, in the face of this opposition, to turn wholly away from nature.

Gen Xers, just starting to come of age, saw the future their parents' generation and the generations before it had gifted them, and they were pissed.

Some channeled their rage into activism. Gen Xer activists took the immediacy and tangible nature of monkey-wrenching and combined it with the high theater of Greenpeace's "Save the Whales" ocean campaigns, tiny zodiacs bobbing and weaving in front of whaling harpoons, the occupational protests of the civil rights movement, and the "run a pig for President" humor of the Yippies, and created a new hybrid form. They placed their activism under the mantle of *direct action*. Described by their parents' generation as a close cousin of sabotage, direct action took the form of weeks-long occupations of ancient trees or chaining oneself to logging equipment to protest deforestation, or guerrilla gardening, or living in human-size cages outside research facilities to protest animal testing. Such protests were staged for the evening news, and more focused on delays than damages. It was a disorganized and decentralized movement that was decidedly not human centric. Central to its philosophy was a change in lifestyle. As a result, the era saw a rise in recycling, vegetarian and veganism, the use of animal-cruelty-free products and mass transportation and bicycles, and calls for pesticide-free and non-GMO foods.

Direct action as practiced by these environmentalists would eventually become a worldwide norm, but it was born in the western United States, and particularly in the forestland along the Applegate Trail, which was ground zero for the fight over old growth. That fight developed more than just the radicalized wing of environmentalism, it also created a mainstream movement that focused in on particular, individual issues, species, or locations and leveraged the system's own rules and regulations against itself. From the Greenpeace whales to the Spotted Owl, activist groups learned they could use a single protected species or land provision to gain protection for entire swaths of land. The legislation that established protections for individual streams, forest areas, or species was complex and mired in rules and red tape that was meant to benefit corporations. Now, activists were finding ways to tangle the system in that red tape, diligently requesting, reviewing, and challenging environmental impact statements, historical records reviews, and long-term studies. Roadblocking. It was effective, but it did little to quell the cynicism and ennui of the generation, which embraced a certain nihilism as epitomized in REM's hit "It's the End of the World as We Know it," Nirvana's "Smells Like Teen Spirit," and movies like *Tank Girl* and *Reality Bites*. And why not? As

Douglas Coupland, who popularized the term *Generation X*, wrote in his book *Shampoo Planet*, that generation and the ones coming behind it, were "never far from the sound of an engine." It was all part of a larger existential crisis, similar to the one that Jean-Paul Sartre described as facing the young men choosing to stay and help family, or go to battle during the World War II. Allow large-scale extinction and decimation of the natural world, or give up on the American Dream in all its consumptive, chemical glory. Along the Applegate Trail, the choice was simple: stop cutting down four-hundred-year-old trees or preserve the livelihoods of the region's human occupants. Gen Xers had a choice: north to trees, or south to gold.

For a moment, it seemed as if Generation X, raised as they were with an eye to health, the environment, and racial and social justice, could choose trees and maybe even win. But no. The backlash from their boomer parents was swift, surprising, and ultimately hypocritical in the eyes of their children. While their kids had been radicalizing, their parents had drifted far, far away from their summer of love and right into the arms of 401k-driven anti-environmentalism. Anti-environmentalism opposed regulation of natural resources and management of public lands, which they saw as sources of financial gain, and derided any moral, spiritual, or other forms of value assigned to the environment. It was popular among those who called for less government regulation of all kinds, those with Libertarian ideals, and corporate America (for obvious reasons). It also thrived in rural and wilderness-adjacent communities that had, over time, adopted an ideology of radical individualism based on pioneer legends. These people raged against bureaucracies and derided all forms of "tree hugging." And they voted. Ultimately, it was a numbers game. Tiny Gen X never had a chance.

As the millennium approached, direct action, now classified as domestic terrorism, went the way of physical maps, which were quickly being replaced by geographic information systems (GIS). GIS systems provided the ability to collect and analyze massive amounts of spatial data making it not only mappable but searchable and easily combined and manipulated. It allowed for all kinds of new understanding of patterns and relationships across landscapes. It transformed the way we conceptualized information. We were suddenly able to fly over, across, and into the world around us. From that perspective, one could see clearly the stark contrasts between the deep green of ancient forests and the dusty browns of clear cuts and compare the rate of regrowth in managed plots with different soil types or aspects to the sun. But it was part of a larger digital movement that removed us from the landscape, forever abstracting the natural world. From this new digital perspective, Americans bifurcated reality into digital and physical space and increasingly chose digital spaces. To achieve this, they retreated indoors. Car culture, once a means of outdoor recreation, morphed into a monotonous requirement of American life that increasingly valued busyness over leisure. America became a Prozac Nation. Fossil-fuel demand skyrocketed, and oil became a symbol for, and cause of, war. Nature did not just end; it was forgotten.

And then there was the issue of the millennium. Millenarianism has always been a part of American thinking. The Mormons, Seventh-day Adventists, and Jehovah's Witnesses were rooted in beliefs about the end times, the rapture, and the return of Jesus that were associated with the end of the millennium. With the actual event rapidly nearing, the Christian right, especially evangelicalism and fundamentalism, surged. This, paired with the predicted doom of global communication systems related to the year 2000 (Y2K), drove a wave of apocalyptic thinking. To many, it seemed as if the sky was falling.

SIGNPOST

In the twentieth century, the term wilderness shifted from an existential, philosophical idea to a legally binding term. "A wilderness, in contrast with those areas where man and his own works dominate the landscape, is hereby recognized as an area where the earth and its community of life are untrammeled by man, where man himself is a visitor who does not remain. An area of wilderness is further defined to mean in this chapter an area of undeveloped federal land retaining its primeval character and influence, without permanent improvements or human habitation, which is protected and managed so as to preserve its natural conditions and which (1) generally appears to have been affected primarily by the forces of nature, with the imprint of man's work substantially unnoticeable; (2) has outstanding opportunities for solitude or a primitive and unconfined type of recreation; (3) has at least five thousand acres of land or is of sufficient size as to make practicable its preservation and use in an unimpaired condition; and (4) may also contain ecological, geological, or other features of scientific, educational, scenic, or historical value."

—16 U.S. Code § 1131, National Wilderness Preservation System

SIXTEEN

TRAIL STORY: OCCUPY BALD MOUNTAIN

In the spring of 1984, a man name Lou Gold set up camp atop a mountain in southeastern Oregon and refused to leave. They called him the Hermit of Southern Oregon and for the next twenty years he occupied the top of Bald Mountain in what is now the Kalmiopsis Wilderness Area for at least four months each year. Today, it is the largest remaining area of old growth in Oregon.

The Siskiyou National Forest was created in 1907, just two years after the creation of the Forest Service. Its boundaries fluctuated from the start and still do; the current iteration is combined with the Rogue River National Forest. In 1964 a portion of the forest was granted protected status with initial passage of the Wilderness Act. Fifteen years later, that portion, the Kalmiopsis Wilderness, became the flash point for what would come to be known as the Northwest Timber Wars.

The Rogue-Siskiyou Forest, and the Kalmiopsis in particular, sits at a geologic convergence, the suture point between the coast range to the west and the Siskiyou Mountains to the south. There, a mélange of bedrock types, the sandstones, limestones, and shales of the coast range's uplifted seafloor collide with ancient terranes from other parts of the world that have been folded and metamorphosed over millennia. The weather reflects the complex topography, as sunlight and evaporated water wend their way toward each other through the steeply eroded mountains. Temperate rainforest along the coast gives way to alpine forests inland. In some areas annual rainfall totals exceed 150 inches, in others, barely forty. It is the same rough and rugged kind of territory that trapped and confounded travelers on the Applegate Trail in the 1800s—high, steep mountains with plentiful winter snows and piercing summer sunshine. The Applegate River, named for the brothers, drains its crystal-clear waters from the forest. That river, and many of the rivers in the area are known for hosting a broad diversity of fish species.

The ecology is no less variable. The Siskiyou is home to an astonishing number of plants and wildlife that is considered to be the most diverse forest ecology in the west, perhaps even the world. Redwoods stand alongside Port Orford cedars, yews, and sugar pines, twenty species of conifers all told. Throughout the area, the underlying rocks conspire with the unique hydrology of the mountains to create microecosystems. In several places there are broad swaths of wetlands perfectly suited to host the Darlingtonia, a rare and prehistoric-looking carnivorous plant. Before the arrival of white people, the rich ecological diversity sustained humans for at least ten thousand years.

After that, it was Indian War territory. For most of the rest of its modern history, it was mining country. The first gold in the area was found in 1851, but over time it produced nickel, copper, and chromium in abundance too. Sometime after the Great Depression, long after the peak of lode and hydraulic mining had passed, it became World War country. Some of the only known bombings on the American mainland during World War II occurred there, though to little fanfare, as the area remained largely unpopulated. Throughout the war, the Japanese had wanted to use the forests of the Pacific Northwest as a military target, not because of the potential threat to infrastructure or the general public, but as a means of terrorism. Their idea was to use bombs, either dropped by balloons or planes, to start wildfires. On September 9, 1942, they did just that, sending a pilot in a small plane over the Siskiyous to drop two bombs in an isolated portion of the forest. That effort (and most subsequent ones) failed; in that instance it was due to the watchful eye of a lone forest ranger in a remote fire lookout who spotted the plane, heard the bomb, and set off on foot with one other ranger to put out the flames.

But let's go back to 1983. Because by 1983, established conservation groups like the Sierra Club had been battling the Forest Service over forest management and the establishment of wilderness areas for decades. Mostly, they were losing. Since the Applegates and their road-scouting team punched through the Siskiyous one thing had remained constant, people had trickled in, but timber had streamed out, millions of board feet a year. In 1983 close to ninety percent of the temperate forests of the United States had already been logged, some several times. Through wilderness designation, conservation groups were fighting to preserve the last remnants of the oldest forests, those on the most remote and difficult of terrains. One of the things that's important to know about wilderness areas is that they are, by definition, roadless. That is to say, the legal definition of wilderness in the United States is deeply linked to those mid-nineteenth-century visions of western paradises, untouched by the hand of man.

By law, wilderness, in order to be wilderness, must be devoid of humanity, especially that most twentieth-century marker of it: roads. And at that time, there was no means of conversion. Once a place has been developed, it will always have been developed. Never underestimate the power of a humble road.

While millions of acres that fit the wilderness requirements had been set aside, protected land area still constituted only a small fraction of public forests. The situation, as seen by the timber industry, was largely administrative. With the blessing of the Forest Service, who up until the 1970s had seen itself largely as the manager of an agricultural product, not land, big timber had devised a workaround. It had become common practice for logging operations to construct extensive roads through undesignated roadless areas, ostensibly to reach a remote though often limited timber tract. The road would then make the surrounding areas along its entire stretch ineligible for wilderness designation. In this way, they ensured the future harvest of public lands that could no longer be designated as wilderness.

When such a road through the Kalmiopsis failed to be blocked by lawsuit, the antiestablishment Back to the Landers who had congregated in southern Oregon applied their experiences from the civil rights and antiwar movements and showed up in person. These activists, loosely affiliated with a group calling itself Earth First, were inspired by the personal action directives of deep ecology and the practice of monkey-wrenching as popularized by old Ed Abbey. Combined, they would come to call it taking direct action. At the time, they called it being pissed. The proposed road was to pass over the top of Bald Mountain, just six inches from the existing wilderness boundary, and terminate at an old-growth tract slated for harvest. At that time the area consisted of a 150,000-acre unprotected old-growth stand surrounded by an additional 250,000 acres of roadless, undesignated forest, the North Kalmiopsis Roadless Area, in turn surrounded by the 1.3-million-acre Siskiyou National Forest. Bald Mountain was the center of the bull's eye. All those mills that had seemingly been along the Applegate Trail forever were still calling out for the ten-foot-wide trunks of ancient trees. Road construction began as scheduled.

In April 1984, Les Moore, a bulldozer operator working on the road, found his progress blocked by four men. "Hippie types," he said, had appeared in front of him and wouldn't get out of the way. He gestured. He yelled. He called them "fucking communists." They held their ground. One yelled back that he was a registered Republican. Increasingly frustrated, Moore pushed the rig threateningly toward them. But they just locked arms at the elbows. He backed up. Then he pushed a moraine of dirt toward their feet. Again. And again. Finally, he climbed down and went to call the sheriff, or whomever it was that dealt with obstinate, tree hugging, dirt worshiping, Republican hippies. Eventually, the authorities arrived and arrested the men. Moore returned to work. "Nothing like this had ever happened in Oregon's timber country," he would tell the press after the incident.

After that day, things like that started to happen in Oregon's timber country all the time. It was clear that something fundamental had transpired, that a new kind of protest had emerged, one that was specific in time and place and uniquely visceral. By the end of the summer, it had become a movement, pitting frontline workers' livelihoods and corporate profits against activists' bodies. Despite their remote locations, some of the blockades made national news when protestors chained themselves to equipment and road gates, and conflicts with loggers reached boiling points. The confrontations grew increasingly violent. The news ran footage of protestors being dragged by their necks across gravel tracts and overrun by log trucks. In one confrontation, protestors were nearly buried alive by an angry bulldozer operator. Dozens of arrests were made, but only of protestors.

Lou Gold was among them.

Gold was a boomer, an emigrant from the east coast, an intellectual and college professor. He taught American Government and urban politics at Oberlin College and the University of Illinois and often told his students that he fantasized leaving the college to "drop out" of mainstream society. And one day, he did just that. By his own account, he had deliberately come west seeking distance from the "world of glass and concrete." He chose that particular corner of Oregon by opening the map and looking for the place that seemed farthest away from humanity—literally just pointing to an empty place on the map and setting out. "What led me to the mountains was a search for my own wholeness," said Gold in an interview nearly five years after his emigration. He was arrested and banned from the forest in 1984, on his first day of road blocking; it was just weeks after his arrival. But with no one to enforce such an order and so much wild open country, Gold returned the next spring, this time to set up temporary residence on the top of Bald Mountain, the center point for the conflict.

There, with a nearly 360-degree view of the embattled forest, he built a makeshift shelter and settled in. Some days, hikers would wander through. Some days, most days, he saw and spoke to no one. After his first season, upon returning to town, he was re-arrested and jailed. In his second season, people began to visit him, bringing him supplies to help sustain his occupation of the mountain. He started fashioning walking sticks and gifting them to his visitors. At the end of his second season, he wrote:

"We stood humbly in the midst of a great natural harmony, and the world, for the moment, seemed in order."

Off the mountain, the media coverage of the roadblocks rallied the support of Oregon's liberal voting base who made calls to elected officials and wrote letters and donated to legal funds. A new lawsuit was filed and a preliminary injunction was issued. Construction on the road stopped.

Then, in October 1984, President Ronald Reagan signed the Oregon Wilderness Act. It created several new wilderness areas in the state but excluded the North Kalmiopsis Roadless Area. In doing so, it blocked it from all future consideration for wilderness designation. Worse, the bill undermined the fragile protection afforded by the injunction and opened the door for the Forest Service to complete the Bald Mountain Road.

But the Forest Service didn't build it, at least not right away. Public sentiment had been changed, and so had the Forest Service's, whose mission had now for over a decade included protection of forestland for recreational purposes—that is, for the enjoyment of the land by people. And the people, Lou Gold most of all, had made it clear that they loved Bald Mountain. Everywhere, a new generation of environmentalists, just coming of age, took note. Direct action worked.

Gold kept his place on Bald Mountain for twenty years. In that time, people, hikers, activists, locals bearing homemade meals, visited him. He talked to them and for a while they would share his mountaintop and listen. For the first decade, in winter, he became a wayfaring storyteller, touring the country to talk to people about ancient forests and the need for their protection.

He preached a unique blend of ecology, socioeconomics and politics, and motivational empowerment, what he called Earth Wisdom & Political Activism, motivated by the belief that action was a "meaningful antidote to despair." He stopped his touring in 1994 when President Bill Clinton instituted the Northwest Forest Plan, which was designed to bring the timber wars to an end, promising to both protect and ensure harvesting of more than 24 million acres of Northwest forests.

In the years of Gold's watch, the Siskiyou, long managed under a strict fire-suppression regime, became known for its massive wildfires, a harbinger of what was to come. As a result, wildfire salvage has become a major source of new-timber harvest throughout the forest, opening vast stretches of land to logging operations. No one seems happy with the Northwest Forest Plan, but the Spotted Owl, the most visible endangered species of the battle, still thrives, the log trucks still roll out timber from public lands, and the Kalmiopsis, Bald Mountain included, is a designated Wilderness Area.

SEVENTEEN

THE FALL OF MAN, 2001–2015

SPUTNIK'S BEEPING SENT WAVES OF FEAR THROUGH THE HEARTS of midcentury Americans, but it was nothing in comparison to the shockwave created by the events of September 11, 2001. The turn of the twentieth century had, in fact, not brought about the rapture, the return of Jesus Christ, or even the demise of premillennial computer systems. Instead, it ushered in a new era of terrestrial fear—terrorism.

On that day, the whole of the United States, the whole of the world, stood witness in real time as airplanes careened from the sky toward the most symbolic of buildings, our modern cathedrals to commerce and war, the pentagon and the World Trade Towers. At ground zero, people made life or death choices. Firefighters ran into buildings as office workers ran out. Some companies evacuated early, some stayed until it was too late. High above the ground, people appeared at the windows on floors above the fires. With no way out, they faced a choice: stay to choke or burn or die in a collapse, or jump. For 102 minutes after the north tower was hit, people chose. With the whole world as witness, they jumped, calmly and with dignity, one after another, in pairs and groups, flying, falling, for what seemed like an eternity. One of those falling people was captured in a photograph, plunging head first, with his arms at his sides, the lines of his body perfectly aligned with the lines of the massive tower behind him. In its elegance, the image resonated with a nation built on choice and individual freedoms. Unable to identify him, news outlets called him simply, "The Falling Man."

At first, the raw humanity of the image, it's beauty and sadness, was too much and other kinds of pictures became the iconic images of that day. People forgot about The Falling Man. With time, though, it reappeared. Now, it is embraced. The Falling Man, has come to symbolize the everyman, the anonymous American, the one who could be any of us, choosing.

The plumes from the fires and collapse debris were, like the towers had been before them, visible from space, from the myriad satellites that now occupied the skies, and from the newly launched International Space Station, the first house on the new frontier. In the decades since the first moon landing, such images, collected from miles above the Earth, had changed our lives and worldviews. In the new millennium, we were able to zoom in, to see ourselves in our own backyards, the nuclear families, the lonely old men, the tidy squares of land all parceled up like all those tiny squares of township and range two hundred years earlier. These most modern of images captured our collective humanity from a different contextual scale. In them, the whole of the American population was minuscule when set against the backdrop of all that land.

On that day in September, we were made even smaller by the enormity of the plumes of smoke rising from our temples. Sure, a theoretical view from above had always been afforded by maps, but the stories those images told—the fictions, fantasies, and truths—even the layers of data added by computers, none of it mattered once you could see the means of your own destruction, streamed from satellite view in near real time. That was the charmed glass through which Americans looked from that day forward. It showed them a whole new kind of uncharted territory, one that would define the postmillennial American experience. This new American experience, the new American normal, was marked by the loss of privacy and other rights, the rise of extremism, never-ending wars rooted in our dependence on petroleum, and shocking tragedy after shocking tragedy fueled by gun violence, extreme weather, and, at last, the end of our abundances.

We all know that far more than buildings and lives were lost on that September day in 2001, though perhaps we have yet to adequately define all that it was that we lost. Surely though, the collapse of the World Trade Towers represented the collapse of something large and intangible. Freedom, most especially personal liberty, certainly fell, and minds were changed, somehow. There was something more insipid, too, something about the way Americans lived, something tied up in fear.

Fear is a curious thing. Driven by the unknown, it causes all kinds of strange behaviors, hoarding, protectionism, lashing out, constant searches for threats and enemies. After the towers fell, Americans engaged in many of these behaviors. In particular, they leaned into anything that would ameliorate: the pleasures of consumption, the security of ownership, the numbing effects of drugs, prescription and otherwise. Bolstered by easy financing, they bought houses, especially in the west, which seemed to provide some kind of safe harbor, even if just by distance. They bought cars, massive, reinforced, and gas guzzling. They bought fast fashion, flat screen TVs, and phones. They bought everything they could until more than half the adults were obese and more than half the households paid for offsite storage facilities. This was not the happy, plump consumerism of the mid-twentieth century. In the new, wholly anthropocentric and survivalist century, Americans bought out of habit and tradition and most of all to fill the hole of fear and fatalism that had been ripped open wide by images like that of The Falling Man.

In this new regime, regulations, especially those that dictated one's mobility, thrived. Airport security lines filled with shoeless travelers, IDs were checked and rechecked, student visas scrutinized. Across the country, America's wildlands saw a coincident increase in developed areas, maintained roads, permits, and rules that in their totality gave the federal government unprecedented authority to, as Louis Warren asserts, police travel across the very landscape that had come to symbolize unfettered American freedoms. And there was something else. It was less tangible than protocols and administrative shifts, something that came from the people, a subtle uptick in patriotic fever, a hard swing of the left to the moderate, safer, center. Radicalism of all kinds was eschewed. Environmentalism, practical and theoretical, got swept up in the shift. All the headline-grabbing theatrics of the radical movement, once inspirational, were now dangerous, destructive, anti-American. Patchouli-wearing granola types were the last thing a population racing toward the normative center wanted to be associated with. Anything that smelled woodsy or environmental became off limits, a sign of softness, woo-woo, communism, or even paganism. Direct action, now clearly defined as ecoterrorism, nearly faded away entirely. People went inside.

Environmental writer Richard Louv defined a new syndrome in postmillennial children—nature-deficit disorder, the tangible consequences of McKibben's *End of Nature* and the inexorable rise of the internet age. Headphones replaced mouse ears. American kids were plugged in, tuned in, and barely on.

Meanwhile, symptoms of a new problem began to emerge: the sudden and obvious onset of global climate change, manifested as a sharp increase in the frequency and power of hurricanes, pronounced droughts, and polar bears swimming hundreds of miles in search of ice. But this clear evidence of climate change did little to shift the hearts and minds of Americans from human-centric problems to the natural world, of which they no longer saw themselves a part. The uptick in regulations and erosion of freedoms hadn't sat well with the ever-decreasing populations of rural communities, those few areas, like those along the Applegate Trail, where the connection to the land and the people was still evident. Nationalism and fundamentalist and evangelical Christianity blossomed, and with them the belief that climate change, and perhaps even the science the "theory" was based on, was a hoax. For many middle-American Christians, natural disasters were consequences of moral decline, the lack of family values, and any number of other perceived social "sins," from abortion to gay marriage. This way of thinking was not, in spite of a surge in mainstream liberalism perhaps best illustrated by the election of a progressive president and his status as the first Black man to hold the position, fringe thinking. In the first dozen years of the millennium, governors of at least three states, Alabama, Georgia, and Texas, held prayer vigils in response to droughts.

Across all belief systems, everyone kept consuming. Microplastics filled the oceans, heavy metals trickled out of mountain streams, landfills filled. The postwar engine that was American consumerism pressed on. Globalization, particularly of consumer goods, had already begun to create a worldwide monoculture. Big-box stores occupied increasing portions of the landscape, restaurant chains dominated the foodscape, and visible branding came to denote value. The response to this monoculturing, among other things, was escapism. For many it was in the form of drugs, especially opioids. For others it was media, or food, or roller-coasters. For some untold number, it was expressed in the form of neo-tribalism. And here is where we get to Burning Man, an art-filled extravaganza held each summer on the dusty playa just north of the Humboldt Sink.

Concerts, shows, parties, gatherings of the tribes, happenings, acid tests, over time they had been called many things. By the late aughts, they could easily be lumped into a broader category of festival culture. Festival culture, and the larger neo-tribalism movement, in America was characterized by cultural appropriation, pseudo-spiritual practices, virtue signaling, elitism, and privilege. People in the twenty-first century turned to festivals in the way they turned to wilderness in the romanticism of the 1800s, in the way postwar Americans turned to it in the mid-twentieth century—as a place akin to a cathedral and close to God. Festivals, with their digitized fantasy worlds, sought to re-create that feeling of import, of communing with something greater, something more beautiful, something more perfect and divine than ourselves or even nature. It was in many ways a futuristic, digitized attempt to return to the garden. It was the colonists arriving to the eastern shore, the explorers seeking a western silk road, the missionaries looking for redemption, the endless search for the promised land. It was history repeating and repeating and repeating, each time with less water, fewer trees, more people, higher temperatures, more roads.

Festival culture in the decade following the 9-11 attacks came to symbolize the commodification of spirituality and the quest for that old notion of ecstatic grace in what was now the post-joy world. It was a rising of the ego and the id, where ordinary people migrated out of the cities to shed the confines and expectations of their daily lives. At festivals, they transformed themselves, pushing against the tyranny of normalcy, against the need to conform. In these invented spaces they practiced weekend warrior spirituality—postmillennial New Ageism, yoga, chanting, and whatever other kinds of rituals had been invented for their consumption. Celebrated as temporary alternative societies, festival culture evolved as both a rejection and an amplification of mainstream culture, a commercial version of the radical left, that would bend at its edges to include many tenets of the newly emerged post-9-11 radical right. Those that were successful over the long-term, like the Renaissance Faires, Oregon Country Fair, or Burning Man, became microcosms.

Like any new society, these events had to create order out of chaos. In doing so, they faced the same questions of authority and power that predecessors like the communes and wagon trains had more than a hundred years earlier. And they had similar struggles with infrastructure, environmental impact, resource use, and population growth as the early settlements and towns and even the communes of the 1970s. Over time, these and other generational changes began to eat away at the original core intention of the movement that mirrored, at base, the Humboldtian concept of the cosmos, the Transcendentalist's ideas of divine ecstasy, deep ecology, and the cyclical urge to go back to the land. Rape culture, pay to play, elitism, pollution, all reared their ugly heads, as did monetization and large-scale spiritual bypassing of environmental impacts and issues as people engaged in the postmillennial frontier in which everything is framed in a scarcity mindset and the underlying idea of burning our own humanity. People loved it. Each year more and more poured out into vast wild spaces to see them transformed into digital paradises that resided someplace between or beyond the wild and the world of man.

The wild and the world of man. Nearly four hundred years later and so much import still rests in that dualistic, colonial, Christian division. Dualism, the separation of man from nature as exemplified and enhanced by digitization, by virtual reality, by wars fought through video games from the desert, by illuminated trees, by the burning of even secular temples, and burning men. What does it mean for us to believe that we are separate from or independent of nature? How does that change our relationship to the natural world? Does it dissolve that relationship entirely? What are the consequences of people receding into built spaces, demanding more and more literal separation from the natural world, like so many RVs across a barren playa? What does our desire to encase ourselves away from nature do to our ability to preserve and protect it, even if we choose to do so only as a matter of our own interests, inclinations, and survival?

Environmental thinker William Cronon, at the end of the twentieth century, suggested that it is inherent in modern environmentalism to cast the situation as a binary, either the world of man or wilderness, because to the mainstream mind, landscape is inherently authentic, while built environments, the stuff of man, lack authenticity. Cronon says, with uncanny prescience, that "wilderness is the natural, unfallen antithesis of an unnatural civilization that has lost its soul." Festival culture, with its ambiguous spiritualities, ecstatic graces, and radical rituals, was a modern attempt to bridge this divide between the fall of man and wilderness, the elevation of the already ideal natural world through humanity's innovation.

Like most ventures west, things did not unfold as planned.

SIGNPOST

The Black Rock Desert is a 300,000-acre area of desiccated flatland located just north of the Humboldt Sink. After the gold rush left the emigrant trails west empty, the area was developed with a small town, Hardin City, whose main industry was silver mining. Since the abandonment of Hardin City to ghost-town status, the area has been used as a test location for rockets and as a time-trial location for motorized land-speed records. It is also the location for the annual Burning Man festival. Today, it is surrounded by designated-wilderness areas.

EIGHTEEN

TRAIL STORY: BURN THE MAN

"There is enchantment in the word Oregon. It signifies a land of pure delight in the woody solitudes of the West...That is a country of the largest liberty, the only known land there is a place to build anew the Temple of Democracy."

—***CLEVELAND PLAIN DEALER***, 1843

SO MUCH LIGHT AND SOUND AND MOVEMENT. EVEN THE DYNAMics of the wind are visible across the empty desert, revealed in the spiraling movements of desiccated clay particles as they are transported across the playa. Usually, everything here is dust and mud cracks. But not always. In those times, everything here besides the dust and mud cracks is built by human hands, hauled in along the long roads that only lead through, not to, this place.

The arrival experience, like that of the early emigrants, is always the same. Turning off the highway, modern, motorized pilgrims pass along a single track of road that cuts across the mudflats. Instead of emigrant mailboxes and desiccated cattle, they pass information signs, arts installations, wanderers, warnings, initiations of *The Rocky Horror Picture Show* variety, and greeters of every variety, making their way to Center Camp. There, according to John Mosbaugh's cosmological consideration of the festival, pilgrims are presented with a choice. They can choose to stay in the world of commerce, of things known and familiar, or continue through The Keyhole into Burning Man. On the other side of that keyhole is a disposable brave new world. The festival, laid out in a massive half circle, passes the pilgrims through art and artifice, fantasy, and absurdity until they reach what author Lee Gilmore calls its Axis Mundi. Axis mundi, historian of religion Mircea Eliade's concept of the "symbolic center of the cosmos where the sacred is said to erupt into the profane and real world." The Man stands on this point, his massive wooden body centered over a golden spike.

There is never any water. If you choose to proceed, you do so at some risk. The weather is always unpredictable, cold one year, dry and hot the next, and often there are sandstorms that last for days. And, with no commerce, resupply is unlikely. You have what you have, especially when it comes to survival essentials.

Inside, the people are dressed as futuristic barbarians—wild people festooned in faux fur, leather boots, neon feathers, body paint, goggles, tutus, sequins, wide-brimmed cowboy hats, and sometimes nothing at all. They ride moving pieces of art, double-decker triceratops, land boats, and curious bicycles. Art is everywhere. Some is static: A huge wooden form of a man's head and torso rises out of the desiccated lakebed as if swimming, ten-foot-high letters spell out the word INSANITY. Some is fleeting: Dancers, magicians, and musicians seem to appear and disappear into the dust, and the air is filled with flights of fancy. Many installations re-create the natural world.

A menagerie of beasts strikes poses; human-size flowers glow aquarium-blue. Taking their cue from the Field Trip, skydivers drift to the ground. One year, at the edge of the playa, a tree is crafted from shellacked wood salvaged from areas burned in recent wildfires along the Applegate Trail. All around, art cars provide transportation to and from the sea of RVs that shine like prairie schooners in the desert sun. One is fashioned as a pioneer house, cut in half to reveal its interior. A giant timber-constructed owl stands alone. Everywhere, people are at play. There are fun runs, salsa dancing, game shows, quizzes, cuddle puddles, and lots and lots of parties. The Man rises up from the center. Some years, stairs lead up into The Man, allowing people to enter and peer up into his cavernous, whale-size belly. From a distance, the white of his wood and the white of the playa dust meld together. At times the sky darkens to almost black as dust storms and thunderstorms move through. The Temple sits opposite him, the whole stretch of Black Rock City between them. At night, everything is illuminated. Someplace, an artificial tree lights up with the glow of 140,000 LEDs. It is rainbow-variegated, each leaf changing color in its own time. The Man is illuminated, the contours of his body visible from the distance.

The tree, the Temple, The Man. The people.

They are there to watch it burn.

Burning Man is the postmillennial offspring of whatever became of all those Renaissance festivals and hippie fetes like the ones where Dennis and Ernie sold their wares. It started in 1986 when Larry Harvey and a friend built a wooden figure of a man and dragged it down to a Bay Area beach on the summer solstice. There, they set their "man" on fire as curious onlookers gathered around them. It started as a form of personal catharsis, but became an annual event, a ritual, a happening, and then something entirely new—, an important international event, a philosophy, a way of life, a vision of the future. For most of its years, it has happened in a stretch of desert just north of the Humboldt Sink, the far eastern end of the Applegate Road connecting the far eastern end to the grassy field that five decades earlier hosted Kesey and the Grateful Dead.

That day, as they sold tickets printed on yogurt labels in an attempt to save the Kesey's creamery, still-idealistic boomers dreamed of a cashless, non-stratified society filled with art and music and connectivity. At Burning Man, some broken semblance of that is created and destroyed in the dry, empty desert every year. It is a built paradise, a microcosm, an artificial and temporary world that returns annually as tens of thousands of participants from across the entire globe flock to it in a massive migration like pilgrims returning to Mecca, like the coots to the Sink. There, they fight the desert conditions, wearing punk goggles inspired by the steam-engine age. There, they take respite from the graying-out of ordinary life and sit awash in digital music, LED lights, and parlor drugs. The event lasts just a week, but it begins months earlier with a few dozen members of a chosen family who gather to plot out the map of the temporary city. They begin with a ceremony they call the ritual of the golden spike. The golden spike is the central survey point for the platting of the city they build and burn down and build and burn down year after year, encroaching farther out across the desert, growing and swelling and electrifying and increasingly blocking out the natural world in the search for freedom, expression, connection, meaning.

Burning Man is not just a party, though for many, perhaps even the majority, it is exactly that. For adherents, it's an ideology and creed, a kind of passageway into a new way of being—beyond economy, beyond class, beyond this level of consciousness. Burning Man's philosophy is codified into the Ten Principles: radical inclusion, gifting, decommodification, self-reliance, self-expression, communal effort, civic responsibility, leaving no trace, participation, and immediacy.

Every year has a theme. In 2017 that theme was Radical Ritual. Radicalism is an important underpinning for the event. As a festival concept, radicalism is most often interpreted as relating to personal freedom, and for the whole history of Burning Man, that was how it had been used. But in 2017 participants were asked to contemplate a contrasting meaning, one that the Burning Man Philosophical Center said referenced "all that is fixed and fundamental in human nature." This, they acknowledged, was a departure from their norm of "absurdity and expression." That year, they asked the masses to deconstruct prevailing ideologies, to question "normal" and "create postmodern expressions of service and civic duty with a common theme of healing ourselves and the planet we inhabit."

It wasn't popular with a largely secular population. A Burning Man survey in 2015 revealed that less than six percent of attendees described themselves as "religious." Still, each year since 2000, a temple has been built opposite The Man, facing into the outer playa, the eternal expanse of the Humboldtian desert, the edge of all that colonial wildness and chaos. The temple is ecumenical and beyond its spiritual implications is used as a place of respite, contemplation, remembrance, and grief—it is common for Burners to bring objects, memories, and offerings to be burned with the Temple on Sunday night, the ceremonial end of Burning Man.

In 2017 a second temple was constructed in Black Rock City, one that took unprecedented dominance over The Man. Until then, The Man had always stood alone, overseeing the entire festival from an elevated platform. Over time, the platform evolved into shapes, like space ships and circus tents, its purpose always serving to heighten the import of The Man, to make him more dominant across the landscape.

In 2017, the year of Radical Ritual, The Man, for the first time, was enclosed. That year, he was nearly entirely obscured from view by the second temple, the Temple of the Gold Spike. It didn't go over well. It was meant to cast him as impossibly large within the space, to inspire awe like early Cathedrals. In practice, participants said it felt like a cage, the confinement and entrapment of The Man, the loss of freedom. People objected. Eventually, a new sentiment gave way. Isn't this place, this piece of land, this point on the map The Man's home by now, they argued? Then why shouldn't he have a physical, built home there? And shouldn't that home be a sacred space?

Every year on Saturday night, they burn The Man.

The Saturday of the 2017 event, the future pilgrims converged at the feet of The Man just as they had for decades. The fires were set, the flames crawled up the fifty-foot figure and curled around its base, spreading. There were safety precautions, loose ropes, barely-there barricades that keep the crowd, some 50,000 strong, a safe distance from flying embers and falling chunks of wood. Volunteers and staff stood sentinel, holding the line. Fire crews were on hand. It was loud and bright and disorienting. That year, as the flames grew into a conflagration, a man came running from out of the crowd, bare chested, long haired, and muscular. His hands were open-palmed, facing in, spread wide with thumbs slightly raised like some runners do. He dodged and weaved, retreating into the masses before sprinting out again, this time with firemen and volunteers in chase. The crowd was reveling, The Man burning. The runner, suddenly moving with purpose, rushed straight into the flames. For a moment, he was illuminated and seemed to fly as he lifted his feet high in the air over burning debris. Finally, he tripped, and disappeared into the flames.

His name was Aaron Joel Mitchell. He was 41 years old, a Gen Xer and child of the boomer generation. In the weeks before the Burn, he had been in Oregon at another festival, Eclipse, where he had just witnessed the first total eclipse of the sun to happen in recent memory in the region. To outsiders, he seemed happy. He was pictured smiling at the Eclipse Festival, radiating golden-sunshine vibes in skin-tight gold lamé pants, covered in gold body glitter and face paint, a Barbie doll tucked into the waistband of his pants. It wasn't the first time someone had attempted to walk into the fire. The first year, when it was still an improvised beach happening in the Bay Area, a woman had walked up to The Man and shaken his hands as they burned.

When Mitchell ran into the flames, there was a collective gasp, but no one besides the rescuers moved. The Man lit up and fireworks came down and The Man kept burning and no one was really sure what it was that they had seen or if they had seen anything at all, and the burn went on for hours. When the structure finally collapsed, the people cried and sang and danced and cheered and kissed like always as they watched the embers of The Man drift high into the air. Overhead, satellites recorded images of the temporary city as the smoke drifted and the dust settled. The next night, Sunday, they burned the temple like they always had. Larry Harvey, the creator of The Man, died a few months later.

The theme of 2018's burn was I, Robot.

NINETEEN

TRUMP CARDS, 2015–2020

MAP SCALE IS THE RELATIONSHIP BETWEEN A DISTANCE AS it is depicted on a map and that same distance as it plays out in real life. Understanding map scale, especially for navigation purposes, requires us to be able to relate the information presented on the map to the information we are receiving from the world around us and to translate between the two using critical thought processes. You could say then, that getting lost or staying found is really about having (or losing) one's sense of proportion.

When Trump got elected, Americans lost all sense of proportion. When COVID-19 arrived, that loss became deadly.

But let's start in 2016. In 2016 virulence was an abstraction rather than a natural phenomenon, a sign of value as fame seekers, Instagrammers, cults of personality, and validation miners competed in the new attention economy. It was a noisy time, characterized by mass shootings, especially in schools, and opioid addiction, which had reached epidemic proportions. Out of this noise rose the Trump presidency.

Trumps supporters were a familiar bunch. They were conservative, often rural, people who opposed government regulation of natural resources and control over public lands. They were the same Libertarians, corporations, extraction industry workers and now poor communities on the edge of wilderness, all of them clinging to bygone twentieth-century values, traditions, and ways of life. These mostly white, Christian voters perceived their lives as being controlled by academic elite, liberal law makers, and special interests that were weaponizing over-funded bureaucracies and convoluted regulations against them. They were the people who veered to the far right after 9-11 and now they were leading the charge to "Make America Great Again" by lashing out at anything they saw as communist and anyone they perceived as "the other." Somehow, they won.

The tone for Trump's tenure was set in the first moments of his presidency when he signed a series of destructive executive orders. His initial target was the environment. One of the very first things he did in the hours after his inauguration was to reverse protections for navigable waters of the United States, effectively ending all wetlands protections in the country. No one seemed to notice. It was downhill from there, as protections for national monuments were lifted, pipelines were approved, and industrial regulations dissolved. Meanwhile, American life began to resemble the ten plagues of Egypt.

What Trump did was revive the fantasy of the Wild West with all its freedom and opportunities but with none of the land or gold to back it up. Perhaps it was an expression of the dark side of the artificial light from all those phones and festivals, an eruption of all the pent-up hate and rage from generations of broken promises, failed ventures, false starts, and corporate greed. Most assuredly, it was the political expression of what happens when the water is no longer drinkable in Flint, Michigan the heart of the automobile age, when science is undermined by blind faith, when organized religion is weaponized against bodies, when "Make

America Great Again" refers to times and ideals so long past they are rendered useless or that never existed at all. It didn't matter that it was a farce. His people were swept up in the rhetoric of the time, a recycling of the old frontier myth in which individuals had no obligations or responsibilities to the community, the environment, or the greater good. Only this time, they also had no promises of gold. Posterity had arrived, and it was bankrupt.

In 2016 the Applegate Trail had some of the highest rates of drought, unemployment, opioid abuse, and homelessness in the country. Portions of the trail lost their libraries to lack of funding. High school graduation rates declined. The log trucks kept rolling. Identity and culture wars raged. Bitcoin and personal data were mined, draining massive amounts of energy resources that relied on hydropower sourced from dwindling waterways. The problems leaked out into natural areas, where campsites turned into dumps and broken-down RVs served as housing. One forest ranger described the situation in a 2021 interview with *Esquire* magazine: "Not to get apocalyptic about it, but when a society fills up with so many problems that they spill over into what was supposed to be the last refuge, you start to wonder where else a person can hide."

The Applegate Trail, like the festivals, was a microcosm. All across the country, the story was the same: Homelessness was on the rise, as were hunger, food allergies, anti-vaccination sentiment, depression, hate crimes, loneliness, and a new radical movement—the alt-right.

The phrase *alt-right* refers to a broad, decentralized, often internet-based movement that values personal liberties and opposes all forms of equality perceived to diminish their narrow concepts of family, power structures, and American values. On the surface, it can sound a lot like the philosophies of the new communalists or post-millennial festival organizers. Robert Spencer, an early influencer of the alt-right movement told *The Atlantic* in a 2016 interview: 'We are really trying to change the world, and we are going to do that by changing consciousness, and by changing how people see the world, and how they see themselves."The difference was, they were going to do it with Trump, not Jesus, Thoreau, Kesey, or even The Man.

It worked. For four years they claimed to be radicals, rebelling against Trump's swamp and the status quo and insisting upon a return to a warped fundamentalist version of the United States, one steeped in colonial values and viewpoints, particularly those of unfettered freedom and dominion over the land. The stock market soared. The wealth gap widened. People kept consuming.

And then, in January 2020, China placed Wuhan, a city of more than 11 million people, into lockdown. In a matter of weeks, everything about the world was different. How and why it emerged, as act of man, nature, or God, was at first a primary concern, but in truth, all roads led back to humanity. Either the virus was intentionally human made and released, as weapon or folly, or it evolved under new ecological conditions resulting from human behavior. The Anthropocene had not only begun, it had entered the Age of Consequence.

It soon became apparent that issues of survival were far more important than blame or historical context. Suddenly, average people were asked to become home epidemiologists, weighing uncertainties and risks and evaluating the veracity of data collection, interpretation, and reporting. Fear returned and was ensnarled in a paranoid atmosphere of distrust and irrationality. As the economy collapsed and lockdowns dragged on for months, the perpetual cycles of misinformation and technology-driven self-reflection—a result of the internet's algorithms handing our beliefs, wants, and likes back to us over and over again like a set of mirrors in a fun house designed to give you an infinity of images of yourself—did their jobs. All remaining sense of proportion was lost and with it, the ability to decipher truth from fiction.

So began years of scarcity, illness, and social disconnection marked by destruction of the body, loss of community, and natural disasters. It was the breaking of the American spirit.

SIGNPOST

In 1883, the Oregon and California Railroad, using land deeded by nearby homesteaders, constructed a train depot and platted a town at the far reaches of the Applegate Trail. Eastern investors had identified the location, with plenty of sun and water, as a potential boom town and advertised it as a prime agricultural location for willing emigrants. For a while, it worked. People came and planted fruit trees to soak up all that sun and water and soon that fruit, exported via the railroad, was building them a paradise. For a time, Medford and the cluster of communities around it were among the nation's fastest-growing towns. Then the orchard industry, awash in product with not nearly enough domestic market, went bust, taking with it the American Dreams of many of the occupants of that familiar stretch of the Applegate Road. History was repeating.

TWENTY

TRAIL STORY: THE MAN WITH THE WIDE GRIN

PHOENIX, OREGON, SUMMER 2018

NEIGHBORS HAD BEEN COMPLAINING FOR WEEKS ABOUT A terrible smell coming from the tiny brick house that sat behind them, but a search of the overgrown property revealed little more than clutter and dust. The police didn't look hard, maybe because of the resident's reputation as one half of a flamboyant and openly gay couple, maybe not. Three times that July they circled the structure, painted brightly pink, and knocked on the door; eventually, they went in, stepping on household debris everywhere, papers and magazines in the front room, a giant pile of laundry in the back bedroom. Dennis Day, the 76-year-old man who lived there was nowhere to be found. They talked to the elderly couple's handyman, who told them Dennis had said he was traveling for a bit. They left it at that.

Phoenix sits on a dry-grass portion of the Applegate Trail between Medford and Ashland at the intersection of two perennial creek beds. Perhaps because of that, it was one of the first places to be occupied by those arriving by the southern route. The town takes its name from the Phoenix Insurance company of

Hartford, Connecticut, but it was originally called the American Temperance Life Insurance Company. It was founded in 1851 during the early American temperance movement and, being true to its name, originally insured only those that abstained from alcohol. It wasn't a winning business model and soon coverage was expanded to include all customers, regardless of the status of their sobriety. With that shift in corporate morality came the name change and eventually the tiny town, so closely associated with the company, took on Phoenix as its official designation.

It is not a place that has lived up to the loftiness of its mythological name. After the Civil War it became a mill settlement, timber and grain, but never anything more. In 1880 it had a population of 277. In 2010 it had crawled to just over 4,500. If it is known at all, it's known as a troubled place, one that harbors armed militias and meth in nearly equal quantities. In 2018 the rate of violent and property crimes in Phoenix was higher than that of nearly eighty-five percent of all other cities-—more than double those of the surrounding area. Law enforcement was stretched thin. Back then, it was not a place with much to offer to anyone outside its cultural norms, with a poorly funded city government that lacked strong leadership, and it didn't have a claim to fame. But what Phoenix *did* have was an aged Mouseketeer living quietly and overlooked in a bright pink house, whether they liked it or not.

In Phoenix, Dennis and Ernie stood out from the beginning, and they liked it that way. Dennis had long described himself as a "militant homosexual," and at the end of the twentieth century, in a time when gay rights and AIDS dominated headlines, the conservative locals bristled. Dennis and Ernie didn't care. They were commonly found at the HomeTown Buffet, dressed to the nines, Ernie in his signature red-velvet fedora, Dennis in a dinner jacket, men's or women's, riding just to the edge of garish. They painted their house a bright shade of near-flamingo pink because they liked it, and didn't mind if it ruffled feathers. They were bucking every inch of the town's entrenched pioneer masculinity standards, and they knew it. The locals noticed. Some loved them for it, others didn't.

In 2004 Multnomah County, the most urban of Oregon's counties, began issuing marriage licenses to same-sex couples, setting off a statewide battle over the issue. When a federal judge ruled that the Oregon constitution allowed for same-sex marriage and ordered the state to honor the licenses, the legislature changed the constitution. Meanwhile, a conservative political action group, the Oregon Defense of Marriage Coalition, started collecting signatures for an anti-gay marriage initiative. It succeeded by a narrow margin, largely due to voters outside urban areas, in places like Phoenix. It was a blow to Oregon's liberal population in general and the LGBTQ population in particular. Dennis and Ernie were appalled. In 2009 they did something about it, marrying in a protest ceremony with several other couples. The protest made statewide news and cemented the local's opinions of the men, for better or worse.

The next few years weren't kind to southern Oregon. The timber industry had never recovered from the logging wars of the 1980s and the Great Recession took a toll on what industry remained. Poverty and drugs began to take over, and homelessness skyrocketed. Dennis had aged out of being able to work, and Ernie, now in his late eighties, was in declining health. They stopped traveling, even to visit family in California, and they left their home less and less frequently. Most of their meals were delivered by Meals on Wheels. Family stayed connected through cards and phone calls and tried to visit when they could. But Phoenix is a long way from anywhere and Dennis and Ernie seemed fine tucked away in their quiet corner of the world.

But by 2018, their house was in disrepair and they weren't able to keep up with the yard work. And Ernie had begun to fall. Dennis, still dancer petite and roughly half Ernie's size, wasn't strong enough to help him and often ended up calling 911 for help. Dispatch logs recorded at least two dozen calls for assistance between 2015 and 2018. They needed help. One of their friends, Kirk Pederson, recommended that they hire a man who had done some work for him to help the couple with the property.

Daniel Burda was a tall, dark-haired man in his early thirties with a history of drug abuse and convictions for robbery, assault, and trespassing. Community members and ex-girlfriends would later describe him as unstable. But he had done some good work for Pederson and was affordable, so Dennis started paying him $100 a day to do chores and help take care of the house. Soon after that, he approached Dennis about trading labor for a place to stay. It was a proposition which with Dennis wasn't entirely comfortable, but finances were tight and Ernie was falling more often, so he opened his house to the somewhat erratic young man.

It worked out for a while, but to Dennis, it seemed clear Burda was using drugs, and his behavior was becoming more and more unhinged. Dennis found it hard to hold him to his word to earn his keep. They argued. Then in July, Ernie fell several times. At the hospital, they determined his condition had worsened beyond what his husband could provide for. They transferred Ernie to an assisted-living facility in nearby Medford.

Two days later, Dennis turned up at Pederson's house. Burda, he said, had been escalating, using meth, and his temper was growing increasingly menacing. Recently, Dennis told him, Burda had knocked him to the ground. "I need your help getting him out of the house," he told his friend. It was Sunday, and the police station was closed, so they agreed to meet again on Monday and take formal action.

Monday came, but Dennis didn't show up. After a few days, the assisted-living facility became concerned; it was unusual for Dennis, a devoted husband, to not visit. They called the Phoenix police and asked for a wellness check. At the house, everything seemed quiet. There was no sign of Dennis, and when they tracked down Burda, he told them that Dennis had gone to visit friends for a few days. When he had been gone for ten days, the neighbors called, worried. It wasn't like Dennis to leave his pets for so long. The police came to the property again. Finding nothing, they put out a bulletin for Dennis's car. Maybe he had needed a change of scene. Maybe he really was just visiting friends. Maybe he had felt overwhelmed by Ernie's health issues and wanted to escape. Sure enough, they got a hit. Just the day before the Oregon State Police had pulled over a couple more than one hundred miles from Phoenix driving a car that matched the description. The couple, residents of Medford, told them they had borrowed it from their friend, Dennis Day. This time, the police opened a missing person's case, though the lieutenant in charge would later be quoted as saying that at that time they really didn't think anything had happened to Dennis, instead believing that Dennis could have been voluntarily missing. "Sometimes people just up and leave, which is not illegal." Said Lieutenant Price, who was in charge of the investigation.

Ernie, suffering from advanced dementia and struggling to remember even the names of friends and relatives, could be of little help, but he seemed to understand that Dennis was missing. Friends became increasingly worried, especially Pederson, who didn't believe Burda's story about Dennis being out of town. "Dennis didn't have any friends that he'd go to visit," he told reporters later. "There's absolutely nobody that would fit that description." There were other reasons to be concerned. A neighbor reported having recently received a letter from Dennis saying that Burda had been mistreating him. Their cats and dog were found wandering the neighborhood. And with time, a smell started to come from the house. Still the police did little.

That's when Dennis and Ernie's friends from the Renaissance Faire scene, most living out of the state, decided to take action and starting contacting the press. Surely people would care that a beloved Mouseketeer, an American icon, was missing. But it was an uphill battle and several weeks before they found a local reporter who would take on the story. That's when his nephew, who lived in Medford, first heard that Dennis was missing and contacted his sister in California.

Horrified that Dennis had been missing for months without them being alerted, his family launched an independent investigation. Someone out there must have seen him at some point, and even if he had just walked away, he wouldn't have wanted his family to worry about him. They pushed for more press, which was met online with a deluge of homophobic rants and trolling, especially at the local level.

The family's efforts paid off. In February 2019, when national news began running stories about a missing Mouseketeer in a small town in Oregon, the scrutiny motivated local police to redouble their efforts. In April, eleven months after he had gone missing, they decided to search the house again, this time with cadaver dogs. There, they found human remains in a nearly unrecognizable state under a pile of laundry in a back room. It took a month for the medical examiner to confirm that it was Dennis and several more weeks for them to finally arrest three people in connection with his death: the couple that had been in possession of his car and Burda. Because of the advanced state of decomposition of Dennis's body, cause of death remained undetermined, though the medical examiner did find that several bones had been broken by deputies when they first searched the home, stepping on his body.

The arrests provided few answers. In questioning, Lori DeClusin told police that she and a friend had taken Dennis's car after an evening with Burda had gone awry. She said that Burda had been using meth and had grown agitated and violent, so they had left in Dennis's car. But she swore that she hadn't seen Dennis in the house that night and knew nothing of his disappearance. There was no way to prove if her story was true. No neighbors had seen or heard the women arrive or leave with Dennis's vehicle, and no one had called the police regarding an overheard dispute.

Burda was forthright. He told police that he and Dennis had argued, that he had thrown Dennis to the ground, and that he hadn't gotten back up. He also described what he did after Dennis fell, how he hid the body under a pile of clothes and went about his business, cleaning and airing out the house over and over again to get rid of the odor, which, as he put it, "smelled like death." When the investigators finally got around to pulling Dennis's bank records, they discovered that Burda had used his debit card at least eighty times in the weeks immediately following Dennis's disappearance.

That's when they took action. They arrested Burda and charged him with second-degree manslaughter, second-degree abuse of a corpse, identity theft, and fraudulent use of a credit card. But a mental health review found him incapable of standing trial and instead of facing his charges he took Kesey's proverbial flight to the cuckoo's nest and was committed to the state mental hospital in Salem, where he was to remain until deemed fit for trial.

In the hearing, Burda called the charges "messed up" and insisted that without evidence, there was no case against him. He was right. With no cause of death and little physical evidence the prosecution was left trying to prove not so much that Burda had killed Dennis, but that he had allowed him to die by not taking action to prevent it. To make their argument, they tried to use witnesses that had also interacted with Burda to establish a pattern of predatory behavior toward elder, male members of the community. "They all get to know Mr. Burda in a similar time, in a similar fashion. The relationships all ebb between starting in a professional manner and developing into a personal one," a member of the prosecution's team argued. Pederson, the friend who had recommended Burda, and to whom Dennis had gone for help in his final days, had ended his own relationship with him when, he said, "he was out in the yard with a knife in hand waving and ranting to it to the heavens."

In July 2020 Burda was determined fit for trial. In early motions, his attorney took advantage of the lack of physical evidence and seized upon the town's tiny, disinterested police department's bungled investigation, arguing that the prosecution's case rested on inadmissible evidence. At first, they won. No jury would hear of Burda's history of exploitation and violent behavior, the admissions of guilt he had made to interrogators, nor even the recording of a 911 call Dennis had made seeking help evicting him. Burda was ordered to be released under GPS supervision.

Ernie passed away in late 2019, without Dennis at his side. In September 2020, while most of the world sat in some form of COVID-19-related lockdown, an unprecedented dry, hot wind blew in from the east. Before the end of Labor Day weekend massive wildfires would engulf broad swaths of Oregon's forests along the Applegate Trail, taking advantage of the accumulated tinder from years of fire suppression by the forest service and favoring the monoculture and smaller trees of previously logged areas.

The night the fires started, winds exceeded forty miles an hour. In the rural communities closest to the blazes, people were awakened in the middle of the night by firefighters banging on their doors yelling for them to "Get out! Now!" People left with nothing but their house keys, abandoning animals, valuables, entire lives. For two weeks the region held its breath, hunkering down inside under the eerie glow of a permanent sunset, the sky so filled with smoke it obscured the shapes of even nearby houses. Quarter-size embers floated to the ground dozens of miles from the flames. Even residents of Portland were forced to pack bags as the fires, some of them it was soon determined, started by humans, worked their way toward cities. Across the state, more than 2,800 structures were lost in the fire. Two years later, people were still struggling to repair the damage. One of the largest complicating factors of the cleanup was the chemical contamination of the sites from household and industrial sources. The American Dream, lost.

The fallout from Dennis's disappearance and death, what really happened and why it took so long to find out, continued for years. With time, successful appeals allowed more evidence to be entered in the criminal case against Burda. While it seemed clear he played a role in the events of Dennis's death, the extent to which drugs, mental health, intent, or malice also played roles has never been satisfyingly determined. Likewise, the role of the police in the prolonged saga remained under scrutiny. Dennis's family filed a lawsuit alleging mishandling of the investigation. Both the criminal and civil cases remained unresolved in 2023.

Dennis was deeply loved by the people who knew him and many people who felt they knew him through his time as a Mouseketeer. Memorials and tributes to Dennis are uniform in describing him as a shining light, an inspiration, and a kind soul. The kid with the mouse ears. The grown man with the wide grin. A treasure. Somebody's favorite Mouseketeer. But by the larger world, Dennis had been treated much the same way the land across the Applegate trail has been, scoured for what resources could be had, then set ablaze once the shine wore off, the trees ran out, and the wells dried up.

According to friends, Dennis had a guiding mantra: "Don't justify it, do it." It's a sentiment that stands in stark contrast to the lack of action of the population along the Applegate Trail in particular and Americans in general in the face of so many clear existential threats, a clear admonition to those who fail to act. It remains to be seen what will rise from the ashes of Phoenix's 2020's fires, but it would be wise to follow Dennis's advice.

TWENTY-ONE

THE WAY FORWARD

"Wilderness is for people to connect to that spirit that runs through both the wild in nature and the wild in themselves.... I think spirit strives for survival, and it strives for connection."

—SUSAN APPLEGATE, 2019

MAPS CAN'T TELL YOU WHICH WAY TO PROCEED, BUT THEY can tell you a lot about the terrain you find yourself in, how it came to be the way it is, the story of the land as expressed in its contours. In mapping, contours are expressed as lines of equal elevation that separate higher points from lower points. Contour lines are different from other lines on maps in that they never intersect or abruptly terminate but are continuous across the landscape—you cannot be in two elevations at once. Topographic maps use these lines of equal elevation to depict the shape and elevation of the land, the soil and face of the country. Even with the best of maps in hand, you must plot your own way forward. And that, my friends, is the situation in which we now find ourselves.

The stark contours of the second decade of the new millennium—hate, natural disasters, and COVID-19—did not prove to be The End Times, but they did bring us to a crossroads. Now, like so many before us, we stand like pilgrims in the desert and a face a decision. Ours is a collective battle over truth, over science, and over our own ability to face the consequences of our previous decisions. What we're finding is that issues and minds are clouded, that to some degree we have been swept up in a mass mental health crisis. In evidence of this crisis, we send children into schools without masks to face shooters we cannot summon the courage to confront. We crank air conditioners during heat waves, burning the very same fossil fuels that cause the temperatures to rise. We fill our oceans with plastics as fast or faster than we deplete them of fish. We venerate the beauty of "wild" spaces on social media while spending the vast majority of our time indoors. Perhaps most ironically, we conflate horse dewormer and Clorox with medicine while rejecting the very kind of medicines that allowed us to inhabit and decimate The West and bring about the demise of its Indigenous people. We insist on "normalcy" regardless of the consequences. We suffer. The natural world suffers with us.

Humans are not the first things to have disrupted the natural order of the world. Volcanoes and earthquakes, meteors, ice ages, and microorganisms have all wreaked havoc, and the world has continued. But it could (and has) been argued that no other species has had such a broad or profoundly negative impact on global systems, and certainly not in such a relatively short period of time. It is a trend that seems certain to continue. There are more people than ever occupying the earth, over 7.8 billion in 2023, and our consumption of resources and production of toxic and ecosystem altering substances has grown along with us, fueled in large part by the exportation of Americanism. According to Alan Durning, more goods and services have been consumed by humanity since the 1950s than in all of previous human history combined. And, Durning argues, it doesn't seem to have improved our wellbeing. There's plenty of evidence to support his thesis. Reported happiness, base-level security, and life spans, are all in decline.

Recognizing this connection between the environmental problems and challenges of our time and human health and wellness is important. In the past, our attempts at environmental remediation have reflected our continued attachment to dominion, our ongoing belief in our separate and superior standing in the natural world. Our stance toward nature invariably affects how we live—that we have understood since we first drove west in search of gold. But what history has shown us is just how closely tied our fates are to the fate of our surroundings, how we reflect and amplify the human condition onto the world around us, and how the state of nature, when impaired, impairs our own health. This is because environmental issues are inherently issues of both the body and the spirit. For as long as we respire, as long as we continue to be made from earth materials, our bodies and breath, our spirits, will remain connected to the natural world. Unfortunately, politics and old ways of thinking are preventing us from taking appropriate action. Still, it is clear that we have reached a place of great awakening, thrust by plagues, scarcity, fire, and floods out of our magical thinking about the future. Sadly, it is an awakening born out of fear in response to unprecedented changes in our environment. But it is an awakening. What follows this awakening, any awakening, surely must be different.

So here is where I, like the Applegates turning emigrants towards their new road, tell you what I know of a better path. It will not be easy. Our survival, our path forward, like survival on the trail, will be fraught with danger, hardships, and sacrifice, and it will hinge on the stoic resilience of each of us as individuals, the true American Spirit.

To build a future that is worthy of hope, we need a new environmental cosmology for the postmillennial era, one that acknowledges that the old dualistic paradigm that separated humans from the rest of nature no longer serves us and embraces a new paradigm of connectedness and radical egalitarianism. As we've seen through our lens of the Applegate Trail, this new cosmology is not just mandated by our current circumstances, it's backed by history and science.

What will this postmillennial environmental cosmology look like? If done properly, it will be rooted in radical love and uncommon generosity. It will look like a deeply personal and visceral shift in how we approach and integrate lifestyle, health matters, economics, and social justice into our lives. In this re-yoking of humanity to the environment the defense of nature will be, must be, deeply connected to the defense of and preservation of the self and one another. In practice, this new cosmology will be filled with the very best of what was sought in all those journeys west: immersion in outdoor spaces, education and rejuvenation of the body, reconciliation and restoration of the spirit, manifestation and a return to the physical world, and wonder, the essential nourishment of the soul.

First, we have to emerge from the digital space into the physical space. We have to go outside. The natural world is good for us, and it can and must become a sanctuary. Immersion in the natural world, the building of outdoor skill sets, increased accessibility to those spaces, conservation of public lands, the de-stigmatization and de-masculinization of the outdoors, and the embracing of urban wildlands and home-space wildernesses all are important to our journey. Perhaps more importantly, we have to send kids outside. We have to send them outside and that time outside should be considered an integral part of their education. These kids will need to be resilient and adaptable and able to innovate in ways we can't yet dream of, so we need to teach them curiosity and problem solving in addition to scientific and emotional literacy. To do that, we have to change our definition of education which should be seen as the acquisition of a living skill set rather than just amassing a collection of information.

But information is important too. Science should be funded. Scientists and science as a practice should be respected and believed and trusted, as should traditional ways of knowing and the keepers of that knowledge. Other kinds of knowledge, self-reliance, survival, and life skills, so essential to the pioneers, should be returned to places of value, because it is only from a place of relative security that we can ever hope to achieve rejuvenation.

The goal is not simply to survive or sustain, but to thrive. We should aim to restore the world's, and our own, vitality. To do that, we need to invest in rejuvenation in all its myriad forms—habitat restoration, food network security, preventative medicine, decreased pollution and carbon footprints, sustainable resource extraction, living wages, and egalitarian resource distribution.

At a more basic level, we must blur those old colonial lines between humanity and the environment and embrace radicalized self-care as a form of protection of the best interests of all things. To do that, we need to take care of our most immediate environment: our bodies. Health matters like diabetes, asthma, and cancer must be linked to matters of commerce and way of life like sustainable agriculture and clean, low-impact technologies. Mental and emotional health must be seen as linked to individual health as well as larger social issues—inequities and injustices rooted in systems designed to extract resources and dominate land and people. Moreover, we need to find value in and compassion for our whole selves, not just our bodies.

Compassion for oneself creates compassion for others and for all natural things. It is not a new idea. Socrates believed we must have order in our souls in order to have order and oneness with the cosmos. Part of that ordering of the soul can, and must be, an investment in reconciliation and the making of amends to people and land. Reconciliation requires recognition of harm, extension of rights to all things, the sacrifice of privilege for equality, reparations, and a peace-centered culture. It is hard and potent work without which nothing good or sustainable can be manifested.

For that, we will need to return to a culture of doing and a place-centered lifestyle. Instead of chasing some imagined destiny in the broken promises of an unmapped digital world we can step away from mass production and invest in small-scale, hands-on occupations, industries, and economies. Perhaps most essential is the restoration of the concept of dignity in all work and a high culture of craftsmanship, which will allow us to change what and how we consume. We can and must let go of our hungry quests for gold, digital or not, and instead fund arts and philosophy and wellness and produce a surplus of those things, recognizing that evolution is an imaginative process.

What then, when all this work is done? Then we must return to the proverbial garden and recapture the sense of wonder about the world as it is that has for so long been obscured by fables of new and better promised land, by struggle and loss and failed dreams. We must seek out and grasp onto wonder in all its human forms, ritual, laughter, play, and song and we must invest in our keepers of wonder, our artists, storytellers, dancers, and mystics. Most importantly, we must preserve the largess and diversity of the natural world, that part of the Earth that inspires ecstatic grace.

Only when we've walked this hard road of change can we ask ourselves, where are our lines of equal elevation? How do we wish to contour the future world we live in? We have tried divorcing environmentalism from spirituality, we've tried embracing it, we've tried economics, scare tactics, and valuation. But until we resolve these crises of the human spirit, of the American spirit, we will continue to fail to address or respond to timely and tangible environmental crises. This is the way forward. We are all in possession of lifesaving powers. The actions of individuals matter, your choices matter, and for Americans, the essential choice remains the same: north to trees, or south to gold.

SIGNPOST

In March 2020, as COVID 19 made its way around the world, unprecedented measures were taken to mitigate its impacts on humanity. In the weeks and months that followed, the near entirety of the world locked down in an attempt to stop the transmission of the virus. For a time, we glimpsed the possibility of new paths forward, a golden sunset on our horizon. It was all of us.

TWENTY-TWO

TRAIL STORY: THE QUIETING

IN THE BEFORE TIME, LIKE NOW, HUMANITY AND ALL OF ITS machines and engines roared in their forward press toward development, growth, and expansion. In the before time, the wheels turned and the levers pulled and the world strained at the weight of its own endless desire to build and consume, and none of us thought it could ever be stopped. And then the pandemic came, arriving as a whisper, blanketing the world with silence and slowing the turn of the wheel until even time stood still, days passing like water in a lazy stream. And for a while we sat as stones in that water, allowing the wonder of it all to wash over us in the time we will recall to future generations as "the quieting."

"One day, it's like a miracle, it will disappear," the President told the American people.

During the quieting, we watched the tiny squares of township and range sections, stretched neatly across the face of the country, slowly fill with red dots as the virus made its way inland. It stalled at first at the westerly edge of the Great Plains, but then was spurred fast westward by the press of humanity from the east. Eventually those dots grew and coalesced, overlapping each other and obscuring the effect of the township and range, so obvious now in how we mapped our illness, each dot centered, like a bright red belly, in the middle of the section. The map was reduced to hard political boundaries, with national borders closed and different restrictions in each state, township, and range, and those growing red dots.

An estimated forty million Americans lost their jobs in just the first six months. Millions of businesses closed.

In the quieting, the world changed. Streets emptied of cars. Skies emptied of planes. The oceans emptied of noise. Smog cleared. City lights dimmed. People changed. Without restaurants, people cooked. Without masks, people sewed. With nowhere to go, people walked. They checked on neighbors. Gardens appeared in front yards. Children rode bikes. On the streets, homeless people were allowed to retain their dignity, to claim a space in the world, to not be criminalized for their poverty or drug addiction or hard-knock lives. Overhead, for the first time in anyone's memory, the skies were absent of contrails.

Corporations and governments changed, too. They sent workers home, met customers at curbs, redirected funds toward communities, provided healthcare services, barred evictions, reduced interest rates, and extended debt relief. Fines were issued, quarantines imposed, and curfews enforced. The world waited.

Along the Applegate Trail, dry grasses bent in the wind, whitewashed church buildings baked in the sun, and the Charles Applegate house stood quiet and closed to entry. It had been remodeled over the years but still retained its essential character, low ceilings and broad balconies overlooking the Yoncalla Valley, an area pocked by the ravages of the drug war, spotted with abandoned farmsteads, the water contaminated with mercury and other heavy metals from decades of mining in the surrounding hills. Looking at the house from the end of the long lane that leads to it during the quieting, it was hard to know for certain in what year one stood, if time had passed at all.

But time had passed. The original Applegate Trail, now a paved but aging Highway 99, lies a quarter mile to the west of the house. A parade of power lines follows its track. It is paralleled a short way to the east by a still-active rail line, marked from a distance by the small wooden T-poles and ragged wires of the now-defunct telegraph lines. Just yards beyond the rails, cars and trucks roar past on the interstate highway. A row of cell towers overlooks them all from atop the nearby foothills of the Cascades. They are the marks and monuments of history and progress, signs of the time.

And what a time it was. For many it was a time of fear and inaction, tumult and grief and terror that played out not in the streets but in their own living rooms, a disaster set against the blue light of millions of screens. In those days, people took solace in geologic time, in discussions of scale and risk and uncertainty. The kinds of things you learn about from interacting with maps or studying earth science. The kinds of things geologists think about, like extinction, catastrophism, collapse, and recovery.

During the quieting, we learned that we are vulnerable. It was easy to see just how closely tied our fates are to the fate of our surroundings, how we reflect and amplify the human condition onto the world around us, and how the state of nature, when impaired, impairs our own health. It was easy to see how we are all butterflies of a sort, capable of causing hurricanes with a flutter of our wings. And it became easy to see that the old ways of being, the old systems and ways of thinking, would not serve us from this place in history. Why? Because in the past, our attempts at environmental remediation, rehabilitation, and even conservation reflected our continued attachment to our own dominion, our ongoing belief in our separate and superior standing in the natural world and even among ourselves. "It's something we have tremendous control over," Dr. Fauci told us. "It is how we respond to that challenge that's going to determine what the ultimate end point is."

In those early days there was a sense of people keeping time, of some kind of searching for meaning or purpose that might take hold. Soon, hundreds of thousands of Americans were dead, and we watched as police officers took the life from George Floyd's body in an agonizing eight minutes that, like all time in the quieting, seemed to stretch out in front of us forever. The protests raged for weeks, people lying in the streets, their bodies prone on the summer sun-warmed asphalt of the bridges.

And then, with swiftness as summer came to a close, a bursting forth. People emerged, convinced of immunity through privilege, faith, denial, or will. The virus followed, changing, adapting, spreading, and growing stronger. In September great, dry winds blew and fires raged down forest valleys, bringing smoke so thick that neighbors lost each other's houses, even in the cities. The air itself left. For weeks people again sheltered inside, unable to breathe or move. This time, no one argued about wearing a mask. Each day they rose to look out the window to see if the winds had changed, if rain had come, but for what seemed like an eternity, the fires raged on.

It seemed like the election would never come. When it finally did, the people sat and waited, first nearly for days as the votes were tallied, then for weeks through lawsuits and recounts and jargon and denial. Meanwhile, Americans turned on one another, on democracy, on decency, until even our most-respected halls were filled with fury and violence. Outside, storms raged and fires burned, sister crises of the same evolving plant. Things began to fall apart.

All the while, the virus evolved, unchecked.

The quieting did not return.

From the now time, it is easy to see what was lost. We had a chance in that time, an opportunity to turn things another way, to grasp another future. Still, it might not be too late.

Perhaps it is still possible to return to the stream of time, to sit as stones and abide and endure and press into our future, seeking out that essential state of wonder that allowed us to see the truth in the first place. Simple wonder, the wide-eyed fullness that arrives with newfound possibilities, a potent tonic for the spirit—the gift of the quieting.

Because what we learned from the quieting is what is possible from humanity, the lengths to which we can go, the sacrifices we can make for our own sakes and the sakes of others. What we learned from the quieting is that the engines—of commerce, busyness, consumption, oppression, waste, pollution, expansion—can be turned off. In that time, as a human collective, we almost succeeded. Then, we just we let it slip away. And for what? A haircut, Sunday brunch, a weekend at the beach, a beer with friends, profit, power, pride. No reason good enough.

We know how we got here and now; we know what we are capable of doing. We have felt the cool water run across our backs. We can return there anytime.

GRATITUDE

All books take a village, even those written largely from the isolation of a pandemic. Without the ongoing support of many friends and family and members of my writing community, this volume would never have come together. I am grateful to everyone who played a part in the development of these ideas and the shaping of them into this narrative. It would be impossible to list everyone who deserves to be thanked, but I attempt that practice of gratitude here anyway.

High on the list of supporters in need of recognition are Pat McDonald and Rachel Bell and their army of interns at Overcup Press who saw the potential in this book from the depths of the first lockdown. Also, Helena Brantley and Red Pencil PR, whose insight and deep reading of my entire body of work helped me clarify my vision and challenged me to find my unifying truths.

Other insight and wisdom were provided by Brendan Omeara of the Creative Nonfiction Podcast, the family of people at the Oregon Country Fair, especially Sarah Chylek and the crew at Dan's Original Burgers, particularly Shawn and Jay, who saw us and never wavered, Papa Bear Placer for his insider's view of Burning Man, and Cynthia Wooten, without whom the Country Fair would never have existed. Eric Alan, whose dedication to the art of gratitude served as inspiration in the darkest days of writing, Shirley (Eric's mom) for showing me firsthand what it took to go back to the land, Marshall Kirkpatrick, for exposing me to radical '90s activism, Bill Sullivan, for his mentorship, longtime dedication to the protection of Oregon wildlands and careful and inspiring maps, directions, and descriptions of many of these wild places, as well as his wonderful recounting of their histories, Bobby and Meredith Snodgrass for making us welcome on their little corner of the Applegate Trail, Sylvia McRae, Kevin Patterson and Roseanne Reynolds, who spoke to me about Dennis Day, Susan Applegate, who provided oral history and a modern perspective on the Applegate family, and Tom Titus for introducing us. Alethea Steingisser and the Geography team at the University of Oregon provided the map of the Applegate Trail included in the front of the book; thank you. Several authors generously provided time and commentary on this work: David Syring, Julia Park Tracey, Peter Stark, Wendy Willis, Faith Kerns, and Tove Danovich. Oregon Literary Arts for their financial support during the earliest days of the pandemic and throughout my career, and to David Wolman, Blaise Zerega, and the entire team at Alta Journal who published early excerpts and helped me bring the Applegate's and Dennis Day's stories to life. Harrison Green-Fishback provided a singularly wonderful alliteration, thanks old friend.

Thanks also to the cooperative and communal families and communities that have inspired, educated, and included me: Koinonia Portland, Breitenbush, Opal Creek, Westwind, Alpha, the Red Raven Follies, Cerro Gordo, Lost Valley, Dragonfly Earth Medicine, and the extended Prankster and Rainbow families.

To the groups and organizations that fight the good fight and help me do that too, the Spring Creek Project, Oregon Wild,

Great Old Broads for Wilderness, the Nature Conservancy, Friends of the Columbia River Gorge, Oregon's Outdoor School programs, Eugene Area Gleaners, the Nature Conservancy, Oregon Literary Arts for their financial support during the earliest days of the pandemic and throughout my career. To Senator Ron Wyden and his amazing team for his continued efforts to establish Wilderness areas and Wild and Scenic Areas and rivers throughout Oregon. My fellow organizers and speakers for the 2017 March for Science in Eugene, Oregon, thank you for holding the line with me.

A very special thanks goes to the dude putting in the physical guideposts along the Applegate Trail, and all the small associations and historical societies working hard to preserve these bits of history.

To my parents, Jim and Pat McConnell, extraordinary people who have nourished and guided my spirit and left me signposts in the wild that will serve me to the end of my journey. I love you.

And to Paul, who is everything.

CRITICAL SOURCES

UNITED STATES AND OREGON HISTORY

Carnes, Mark, and John Garraty, *The American Nation: A History of the United States*, 15th edition, Pearson, 2015

Kelley, Robert, *The Shaping of the American Past, Volumes 1 and 2*, 4th edition, Prentice-Hall, 1982

Library of Congress Presidential Papers, https://www.loc.gov/rr/program/bib/presidents/papers.html

The Oregon Encyclopedia, www.oregonencyclopedia.org

Oregon Secretary of State World War II Archives, https://sos.oregon.gov/archives/exhibits/ww2/Pages/threats-bombs.aspx

The Reagan Library online resources, https://www.reaganlibrary.gov/reagans/reagan-administration/reagan-presidency

Rector, Elaine, *Timeline of Oregon and U.S. Racial, Immigration, and Education History*, CFEE (Coaching for Educational Equity), City of Portland, https://www.portlandoregon.gov/civic/article/516558

Roosevelt, Franklin D., *First Inaugural Address, Saturday, March 4, 1933*, https://avalon.law.yale.edu/20th_century/froos1.asp

Roosevelt, Theodore, *Instructions for Meriwether Lewis, 20 June 1803*, https://founders.archives.gov/documents/Jefferson

Smith, Page, *The Shaping of America, A People's History of the Young Republic*, Penguin Books, 1989

United States Census Bureau, https://www.census.gov/

Watson, Peter, *The Modern Mind: An Intellectual History of the 20th Century*, reprint edition, Harper Perennial, 2002

Zinn, Howard, *A People's History of the United States: 1492–Present*, Routledge, 2015

Zinn, *The Twentieth Century*, Harper & Row/Perennial, 1980

THE APPLEGATES AND THE EMIGRANT TRAIL EXPERIENCE

Applegate, Jesse A., *Recollections of My Boyhood*, Press of Review Publishing Co., 1914

Applegate, Jesse A., *A Day with the Cow Column in 1843*, Ye Galleon Press, 1934

Applegate, Lindsay, "Notes and Reminiscences of Laying Out and Establishing the Old Emigrant Road into Southern Oregon in the Year 1846," *Oregon Historical Quarterly*, vol. 22, no. 1, March 1921

Applegate, Shannon, *Skookum: An Oregon Pioneer Family's History and Lore*, Oregon State University Press, 2005

Applegate, Susan, personal communication with author, 2019

Bassett, Karen, Jim Renner, and Joyce White, *The Applegate Trail—End of the Oregon Trail*, Historic Oregon City and the Oregon Trail Coordinating Council, 1998, https://historicoregoncity.org/2019/04/02/the-applegate-trail/

Brigham Young University, Overland Trails Project Online Archive, www.overlandtrails.lib.byu.edu

Dillenberger, Paul, Bill Heinemann, and Don Rawitsch, The Oregon Trail Game, Minnesota Educational Computing Consortium, 1974

Emerson, William, *The Applegate Trail of 1846, A Documentary Guide to the Original Southern Emigrant Route to Oregon*, Ember Enterprises, 1996

Helfrich, Devere, Klamath County Historical Society, *Klamath Echoes*, vols. 1–15, 1964–78

Hugo Neighborhood Historical Society, *1846 & 1847 Applegate Trail Wagon Companies in Hugo Region*, brochures 1B and 1C of Applegate Trail Fords Brochure Series, *many of the quotes from emigrants are sourced from this document

LaLande, Jeff, *First Over the Siskiyous, Peter Skene Ogden's 1826–1827 Journey through the Oregon-California Borderlands*, Oregon Historical Society Press, 1987

Lockley, Fred, *The Lockley Files, Oregon Journal*, 1923

May, Keith, *Finding the Trail in Oregon: A Guide to Sites, Museums, and Ruts on the Oregon Trail*, Drigh Sighed Publications, 2002

Morgan, Dale Howell, *Overland in 1846—Diaries and Letters of the California-Oregon Trail*, vols. I and II, Talisman Press, 1963

National Parks Service, *Across the Plains, Mountains, and Deserts: A Bibliography of the Oregon-California Trail System 1812–1912* http://www.nps.gov/cali/historyculture/bibliography.htm

National Parks Service, *History and Culture Pamphlet 508: The 1846 Applegate Trail at Manzanita Rest Area*, www.nps.gov/cali/learn/historyculture/upload/The_1846_Applegate_Trail_at_Manzanita_Rest_Area-508.pdf

Oregon and California Trails Association Online Archive, *Applegate Trail*, www.octa-trails.org/articles/applegate-trail/

Oregon History Project, *Narratives Archive*, oregonhistoryproject.org/narratives

The Oregon Trail Center Online Resources, www.oregontrailcenter.org

Paden, Irene, *Prairie Schooner Detours*, Patrice Press, 1990

Parkman, Francis, *The Oregon Trail*, Penguin Books Canada Limited, 1950Public Broadcasting Service Online Historical Content: *The West*, http://www.pbs.org/weta/thewest/people/

Sargent, Alice Applegate, "A Sketch of the Rogue River Valley and Southern Oregon History," *Oregon Historical Quarterly*, vol. 22, no. 1, March 1921

Schafer, Joseph, *Jesse Applegate, Pioneer and State Builder*, 1911

Stone, Buena Cobb, "Southern Route into Oregon," *Oregon Historical Quarterly*, vol. XLVII, no. 2, June 1846

Virginia Commonwealth University, *Social Welfare History Project*, socialwelfare.library.vcu.edu

Walling, A. G., *Josephine County History, in History of Southern Oregon*, Walling Publishing, 1984 http://www.orgenweb.org/josephine/history/hist2.htm

Webber, Bert, *Over the Applegate Trail to Oregon in 1846*, Webb Research Group Publishers, 1996

THE FRONTIER AND THE WILD WEST

Blackstone, Sarah, *Buckskins, Bullets, and Business: A History of Buffalo Bill's Wild West*, Greenwood, 1986

Bruce, Chris, ed., *The Myth of the West*, Rizzoli International Publications, 1990

Drury, Clifford, *Marcus and Narcissa Whitman and the Opening of Old Oregon*, Pacific Northwest National Parks & Forest Association, 1986

Elliott, T. C., ed., "Captain Robert Gray's First Visit to Oregon," *Oregon Historical Quarterly* 29, 1928

Fees, Paul, *Wild West Shows: Buffalo Bill's Wild West*, Center of the West: https://centerofthewest.org/learn/western-essays/wild-west-shows/

Fox, Charles Philip, and Tom Parkinson, *Billers, Banners, and Bombast: The Story of Circus Advertising*, Pruett Publishing Company, 1985

Grossman, James R., ed., *The Frontier in American Culture*, University of California Press, 1994

Rarick, Ethan, *Desperate Passage: The Donner Party's Perilous Journey West*, Oxford University Press, 2008

Russell, Don, *The Wild West: A History of the Wild West Shows*, Amon Carter Museum, 1970

Seidel, Karen, *Life and Death in the Early Days*, www.eugenemasoniccemetary.org

Slotkin, Richard, *Gunfighter Nation: The Myth of the Frontier in Twentieth-Century America*, University of Oklahoma Press, 1992

Wallis, Michael, *The Best Land Under Heaven: The Donner Party in the Age of Manifest Destiny*, Liveright, 2017

Ward, Geoffrey, *The West: An Illustrated History*, West Book Project, 1996

Warren, Louis S., *Buffalo Bill's America: William Cody and the Wild West Show*, Alfred A. Knopf, 2005

WESTERN GEOLOGY, MINING, AND NATURAL HISTORY

Alt, David, and Donald Hyndman, *Roadside Geology of Oregon*, Mountain Press, 1978

The Atomic Energy Foundation, http://www.atomicheritage.org/

Biello, David, "When did the Anthropocene Begin? Nuclear Blasts May Prove Best Marker of Humanity's Geologic Record," *Scientific American*, February 2015

Biggar, Norma, and Frank DeCourten, *Roadside Geology of Nevada*, Mountain Press, 2017

Bunting, Robert, *The Pacific Raincoast: Environment and Culture of an American Eden*, University Press of Kansas, 1996

Cleaver, Benjamin, "Gold in Oregon," *Illinois Daily Journal*, August 1, 1850

Comprehensive Nuclear Test Ban Treaty Organization, https://www.ctbto.org/specials/testing-times/

Gulick, Robert, *Roadside History of Oregon, Roadside History Series*, Mountain Press, 1991

Hasbrouck, Luther, "The History of Gold in Oregon and the First White Party in the Illinois Valley," *Sunday Oregonian*, August 24, 1902, http://oregonnews.uoregon.edu/lccn/sn83045782/1902-08-24/ed-1/seq-21.pdf

Laughlin, Lee, "*Gold in Southern Oregon: Well-Known Pioneer Tells of Discoveries in 1849,*" *Oregonian*, Portland, January 21, 1900

Livingston, Stephanie, "Archaeology of the Humboldt Lakebed Site," *Journal of California and Great Basin Archaeology* 8.1, 1986: 99–115

Meyer, Robinson, "Geology's Timekeepers Are Feuding," *The Atlantic*, July, 2018

Nevada Department of Wildlife, *Humboldt Wildlife Management Area*, www.ndow.org

Pullen, Reg, *Overview of the Environment of Native Inhabitants of Southwestern Oregon, Late Prehistoric Era*, prepared for the USDA Forest Service and the Bureau of Land Management, 1996

Ramp and Norman Peterson, *Geology and Mineral Resources of Josephine County, Oregon*, Oregon Department of Geology and Mineral Industries, *Bulletin* 100, 1979, http://www.oregongeology.org/pubs/B/B-100.pdf

Spreen, Christian, *A History of Placer Gold Mining in Oregon*, 1850–1870, master's thesis, University of Oregon, 1939

Stovall, Dennis, "The Pioneer Days of Southern Oregon," *Mineral Wealth*, August 1, 1904

Subramanian, Meera, *Humans Versus Earth: The Quest to Define the Anthropocene*, Nature, August 2019

United States Department of Fish and Wildlife, *Timeline of the American Bison*, https://www.fws.gov/bisonrange/timeline.htm

United States Geological Survey Bulletin 1857-A, "Introduction to Geology and Resources of Gold and Geochemistry of Gold," 1988

United States Geological Survey Region 9 Resources, https://www.usgs.gov/unified-interior-regions/region-9

United States Geological Survey Region 10 Resources, https://www.usgs.gov/unified-interior-regions/region-10

Williams, Gerald, United States Department of Agriculture, Forest Service, *The First Century* by, revised edition, 2005

ENVIRONMENTAL PHILOSOPHY, REGULATION, AND HISTORY

Alpers, Paul, *What Is Pastoral?*, new edition, University of Chicago Press, 1997

American Masters, *A Fierce Green Fire, Timeline of Environmental Movement and History*, https://www.pbs.org/wnet/americanmasters/a-fierce-green-fire-timeline-of-environmental-movement/2988

Bergen, Frank, ed., *The Wilderness Reader*, University of Nevada Press, 1994

Buell, Lawrence, *The Environmental Imagination: Thoreau, Nature Writing, and the Formation of American Culture*, Belknap Press, 1996

Cazaux Sackman, Douglas Ed., *Wiley Blackwell's Companion to American Environmental History*, Wiley Blackwell and Sons, 2014 *Alan Durning's midcentury consumption statistics are included in this volume.

Cronon, William, *Uncommon Ground: Rethinking the Human Place in Nature*, Norton & Co., 1999.

Emerson, Ralph Waldo, *Nature*, James Munroe and Company, 1836

Empson, William, *Some Versions of the Pastoral: Literary Criticism*, New Directions, 1974

Jamieson, Dale, ed., *Blackwell Companions to Philosophy: A Companion to Environmental Philosophy*, Blackwell Publishing, 2003

Louv, Richard, *Last Child in the Woods: Saving our Children from Nature-Deficit Disorder*, Chapel Hill: Algonquin Books, 2005

McKibben, Bill, ed., *American Earth: Environmental Writing Since Thoreau*, Library of America, 2008, *many of the dates, numbers, and direct quotes from documents and environmental thinkers and influencers were sourced from this compendium

McKibben, Bill, *The End of Nature*, Random House, 2006

Nash, Roderick, *Wilderness and the American Mind*, 1st–5th editions, Yale University Press, 1974–2014

Sachs, Aaron, *The Humboldt Current*, Penguin Random House, 2007

Thoreau, Henry David, *Thoreau on Nature: Sage Words on Finding Harmony with the Natural World*, Skyhorse, 2015

United States Department of Agriculture—Forest Service, *The First Century*, https://www.fs.usda.gov/sites/default/files/media/2015/06/The_USDA_Forest_Service_TheFirstCentury.pdf

United States Department of Agriculture—Forest Service, *Our History*, https://www.fs.usda.gov/learn/our-history

Warren, Louis, ed., *American Environmental History*, Blackwell Publishing, 2003

The Walden Woods Project, https://www.walden.org/

MAPS AND MAPMAKING

Ball State University Libraries, Maps and Cartography: *Map Projections: A Tutorial*, accessed 2020–22

The Future Mapping Company, *Top Ten World Map Projections*, www.futuremaps.com, April 2019

Goodyer, Jason, *Cave Paintings Reveal Ancient Europeans' Knowledge of the Stars*, Sciencefocus.com, January, 2019

Thompson, Clive, "From Ptolemy to GPS, the Brief History of Maps," *Smithsonian* magazine, July 2017

United States Geological Survey Topoview (online maps), https://ngmdb.usgs.gov/topoview/viewer/#4/39.98/-100.06

United States Geological Survey, https://www.usgs.gov/

RAILROADS

Ambrose, Stephen E., *Nothing Like It in the World: The Men Who*

Built the Transcontinental Railroad, 1863–1869, Simon and Schuster, Touchstone Books, 2000

Athearn, Robert G., *Union Pacific Country*, University of Nebraska Press, 1971

Bain, David Howard, *Empire Express: Building the First Transcontinental Railroad*, Penguin Books, 1999

Digital History, *Building the Transcontinental Railroad*, 2021, https://www.digitalhistory.uh.edu/

Golden Spike National Historic Park, https://www.nps.gov/gosp/

Pollock, Steve, *Irish Workers on the Transcontinental Railroad*, https://www.uen.org/transcontinentalrailroad/downloads/G7IrishWorkersTranscontinentalRailroad.pdf

Public Broadcasting System's American Experience, *Transcontinental Railroad*, http:/www.pbs.org/wgbh/amex/tcrr/filmmore/pt.html

The Transcontinental Railroad, https://railroad.lindahall.org/essays/cultural-impacts.html

University of Massachusetts Boston, *Building the World, Railways*, https://blogs.umb.edu/buildingtheworld/railways/the-transcontinental-railroad-united-states/

BUSTER KEATON AND *THE GENERAL*

Angel Fire, http://www.angelfire.com/indie/busterkeaton/Filming.html

City of Cottage Grove Oregon, *90th Anniversary Celebration*, https://www.cottagegrove.org/citymanager/page/general-90th-anniversary-celebration

Cottage Grover Historical Society Interpretive Materials, Events, and Social Media, http://www.cghistory.org

Davis, Nicole, *Why Buster Keaton Is Today's Most Influential Actor*, BBC, 2022, https://www.bbc.com/culture/article/20220121-why-buster-keaton-is-todays-most-influential-actor

Silent Film Locations, *How Buster Keaton Filmed* The General, 2014 https://silentlocations.com/2014/09/26/how-buster-keaton-filmed-the-general/

Smith, Julian, "Buster Keaton's Last Stand," *Alta Journal*, August 2020

IMMIGRATION AND RACISM IN OREGON AND AMERICA

Applied Research Center, *Historical Timeline of Public Education in the U.S.*, http://www.arc.org/erase/timeline.html

Bruce, Ben, *The Rise and Fall of the Ku Klux Klan in Oregon during the 1920s*, Chapman University *Voces Novae*, vol. 11, 2019

City of Portland, *Oregon History*, www.city-data.com/states/Oregon-History

End of the Oregon Trail Interpretive Center, *Timeline of Black History in the Pacific Northwest*, Feb. 2000, www.endoftheoregontrail.org/blaktime.html

Ignatrev, Noel, *How the Irish Became White*, Routledge, 1995

Illinois Labor History Society, http://www.kentlaw.edu/ilhs/cll-64.html

Library of Congress Learning Page, *Immigration Timeline*, http://lcweb2.loc.gov/learn/features/immig/timeline.html.

McLagan, Elizabeth, *A Peculiar Paradise: A History of Blacks in Oregon, 1788–1940*, Georgian Press Co., 1980

New York Historical Society, www.nyhistory.org

Ohio History Central, *An Online Encyclopedia of Ohio History, Northwest Ordinance*, www.ohiohistorycentral.org

Oregon Blue Book, http://bluebook.state.or.us/

Oregon Department of Education, Agency Milestones, www.ode.state.or.us

Oregon Indian Educators Association, http://www.oiea.org

Oregon Secretary of State, *A Matter of Color: African Americans Face Discrimination. Life on the Home Front: Oregon Responds to WWII 21 Mar. 2008,* http://www.sos.state.or.us/archives/exhibits/ww2/life/minority.htm

Oregon State University, Chronological History 1860–1869, http://osulibrary.oregonstate.edu/archives/chronology/chron_1860.html

Oregon's Immigrants' Rights Coalition, http://www.causaoregon.org/about-us/causa-history/

Public Broadcasting Services, *New Perspectives on the West—Events PBS*, http://www.pbs.org/weta/thewest/events/1840_1850.htm

United States Department of State, *Immigration Act of 1924* (The Johnson-Reed Act), http://www.state.gov/r/pa/ho/time/id/87718

DENNIS DAY AND PHOENIX, OREGON

Armstrong, Jennifer, *Why? Because We Still Like You: An Oral History of the Mickey Mouse Club*, Grand Central Publishing, 2011

Bowles, Jerry, *Forever Hold Your Banner High: The Story of the Mickey Mouse Club and What Happened to the Mouseketeers*, Doubleday and Company, 1976

City Data, *Crime Rate in Phoenix, Oregon (OR)*, https://www.city-data.com/crime/crime-Phoenix-Oregon.html

French, Julie, "Same-sex Couples Wed in Protest of Law," *Ashland Tidings*, January 12, 2009

Hill, Amie, "Confessions of an Ex-Mouseketeer," *Rolling Stone*, June 24, 1971

KTLV News, https://ktvl.com/news/local/some-residents-call-for-phoenix-city-mayors-resignation-over-incident-at-medford-protest

Mann, Damian, "City Manager Fired: City Manager Eric Swanson has been fired after three years with Medford," *Mail Tribune*, June 4, 2015

McRae, Sylvia, personal communication with author, September 29, 2020

Medford Mail Tribune reporting on Dennis Day, 2010–2021

Medford Mail Tribune reporting on wildfires and recovery, 2020–2022

Nolasco, Stephanie, "Original Mickey Mouse Club Mouseketeer Dennis Day Was 'Reclusive' Before He Went Missing, Lieutenant Says," *Fox News*, March 5, 2019

Oregonian Reporting on Dennis Day 2018-2020

Rendelman, Rendel, *Audit: Gladstone in Violation of State Budgeting Laws*, Pamplin Media Group, March 30, 2018

MIDCENTURY TO 1970S COUNTERCULTURE

Aquarium Drunkard, *Dead Notes 3: Dark Star, Veneta, Oregon*, 2013, https://aquariumdrunkard.com/2013/07/29/dead-notes-3-dark-star-82772-veneta-or/

Archives West: Hoedads Cooperative Inc. records and newsletters, 1971–1994

Canty-Jones, Eliza, *Hippie Oregon, 1859 Oregon's Magazine*, July 3, 2017, *source for information about emigrant mailboxes and the phrase, "north to trees, south to gold"

Cluster, Dick, ed., *They Should Have Served That Cup of Coffee: Seven Radicals Remember the '60s*, South End Press, 1999

Dole, Mary, curator, *Tie Dye and Tofu: How Mainstream Eugene Became a Counterculture Haven*, exhibition catalogue, 3rd edition, Lane County Historical Museum, December 2011 (exhibition dates: May 8, 2010 to September 30, 2011)

Field, Sam, producer, *Sunshine Daydream* (film), 2013

Maederer, Bruce, John Ross, and Delbert McCombs, *Hoedads 1981–1995*, hoedads.com, 1998

Mother Earth News, 1970–2000

Plagge, Dick, "Where Have Oregon's Communes Gone?" *Willamette Week*, January 1972

Plante, Tom, "Oregon's Own Funky Fair," *Berkeley Barb*, July 18–24, 1975

Prozanski, Suzi, *Fruit of the '60s: The Founding of the Oregon Country Fair*, Coincidental Communication, 2009

Robbins, Brian, *Talking Sunshine Daydream with Ken Babbs: Kesey, the Dead, and Little Kids*, 2013, https://jambands.com/features/2013/09/20talking-sunshine-daydream-with-ken-babbs-kesey-the-dead-little-kids-and-dogs/

Roskind, Robert, *Memoirs of an Ex-hippie: Seven Years in the Counterculture*, Do It Yourself, 2002

Sanford, Jesse, *Gathering Kinds: Radical Faerie Practices of Sexuality and Kinship*, University of California Berkeley doctoral thesis, 2013

Vanneman, Brian, *Searching for Paradise in the Rain: Oregon's Communes and Intentional Communities of the 1960s and 1970s*, University of Oregon Honors College thesis, August 1997

Whole Earth Catalogue, 1968–1997

Williamson, Nigel, "The Grateful Dead: Eternal Sunshine Dreamers," *The Guardian*, October 2013

LOU GOLD

Baker, Russel, "Pied Piper from Bald Mountain. Activist Lou Gold Campaigns to Preserve Ancient Forest in U.S.," *Northwest Christian Science Monitor*, May 8, 1989

Barnard, Jeff, "Oregon Timber Sale Ignites Furor: Environment—One last battle is playing out in the Siskiyou National Forest," *Michigan Journal of Environmental and Administrative Law*, vol. 7, issue 2, 1994

Fahrnkopf, Susannne, *Takilma Tales: The Hippie History of Takilma, Oregon*, Authorhouse, 2014

Friends of the Kalmiopsis, https://kalmiopsiswild.org/

Galloway, Paul, "Hermit in a Hurry," *Chicago Tribune*, May 16, 1989

Gold, Lou, "Ancient Forests: Pure Gold, "Lessons from the Ancient Forest: Earth Wisdom and Political Activism," slides and stories presented by Lou Gold, available on YouTube

Gold, Siskiyou Project 2008 annual report and journal entries (internet archive access only)

Gold, Visionshare blog, http://lougold.blogspot.com/

Hielman, Robert, "When Hoedads Walked the Earth," *Oregon Quarterly*, 2018, https://around.uoregon.edu/oq/with-a-human-face-when-hoedads-walked-the-earth

Kagan, Neil, *Wilderness, Luck & Love: A Memoir and a Tribute, Michigan Journal of Environmental & Administrative Law*, vol. 7, issue 2, 2018

Voice of the Wild Siskiyou, Spring 1998

1980S AND '90S ENVIRONMENTALISM

Abbey, Edward, *The Monkey Wrench Gang*, Harper Perennial Classics, 2006

Broydo, Leora, "At Loggerheads," *Mother Jones*, 1998, https://www.motherjones.com/politics/1998/11/loggerheads/

Broydo, "Mutiny at the Sierra Club," *Mother Jones*, 1998, https://www.motherjones.com/politics/1998/11/mutiny-sierra-club/

Coupland, Douglas, Shampoo Planet, *Scribner*, 1992.

Covill, Christopher, *Greenpeace, Earth First! and the Earth Liberation Front: The Progression of the Radical Environmental Movement in America*, University of Rhode Island thesis, 2008

Curry, Marshall, director, *If a Tree Falls: A Story of the Earth Liberation Front* (documentary film), 2011

Foreman, Dave, et al., eds., *Earth First!* 3, no. 5 (June 21, 1983), republished by the Environment & Society Portal, Multimedia Library, http://www.environmentandsociety.org/node/6843

Institute for Forest Ecology, "The Clinton Forest Plan," *Z Magazine*, April 1994,

https://www.motherearthnews.com/nature-and-environment/dave-foreman-zmaz85zsie

Montieth James, ed., "Endangered Act Moves, But Snagged by Crucial Kalmiopsis Question," *Oregon Wilderness Coalition Newsletter*, 1997

Oregon Public Broadcasting, Timber Wars podcast, https://www.opb.org/show/timberwars/

Scarce, Rik, *Eco Warriors: Understanding the Radical Environmental Movement*, updated edition, Routeledge, 2017

Schrepfer, Susan, "Diablo Canyon and the Transformation of

the Sierra Club, 1965–1985," *California History* magazine, summer 1992

Thomas, J. W., et al., "The Northwest Forest Plan: Origins, Components, Implementation Experience, and Suggestions for Change," Brower Center, 2012, https://browercenter.org/news/todays-environmental-activists-stand-on-david-browers-shoulders/

Woodhouse, Keith, *The Ecocentrists: A History of Radical Environmentalism*, Columbia University Press, 2018

FESTIVAL CULTURE AND BURNING MAN

Burningman.com and the *Burning Man* journal entries:

https://journal.burningman.org/2012/07/black-rock-city/building-brc/the-golden-spike/

https://templeguardians.burningman.org/about-the-temples/

https://journal.burningman.org/2017/03/philosophical-center/the-theme/the-gold-spike/

https://journal.burningman.org/2017/01/philosophical-center/spirituality/radical-ritual-spirit-and-soul/

https://journal.burningman.org/2017/08/philosophical-center/spirituality/perform-at-your-own-risk-what-weve-learned-about-radical-ritual/

https://journal.burningman.org/2017/07/black-rock-city/participate-in-brc/participate-in-radical-ritual/

https://journal.burningman.org/2019/07/black-rock-city/building-brc/once-more-into-the-dust-2/

https://journal.burningman.org/2017/07/black-rock-city/tales-from-the-playa/coyote-nose-two-strikes-and-the-golden-spike/

https://www.burn.life/blog/aaron-mitchell-deserves-our-empathy

Dinham and Graham, "The Man Who Ran into Flames at Burning Man Has Died," *The Daily Mail*, https://www.dailymail.co.uk/news/article-4848026/Man-ran-flames-Burning-Man-festival-died.html

Gajanan, Mahita, "How Music Festivals Became Such a Big Business," *Time* magazine, August 2019

Gilmore, Lee, *Theater in a Crowded Fire: Ritual and Spirituality at Burning Man*, University of California Press, 2010

Harvey, Larry, *Participate in Radical Ritual*, Burning Man Project, July 5, 2017

Perez-Banuet, Tony "Coyote," *The Gold Spike*, Burning Man Project, March 7, 2017

Taylor, Alan, "Photos from Burning Man 2017," *The Atlantic*, September 2017, https://www.theatlantic.com/photo/2017/09/photos-from-burning-man-2017/538809/

THE TWENTY-FIRST CENTURY

Blevins, Jason, "Fewer Americans Participate in Outdoor Recreation," *Colorado Sun*, January 2020

Davis, Wade, "The Unraveling of America," *Rolling Stone*, August 2020

Egan, Matt, *Billionaire: Facebook Is What's Wrong with America*, CNN Tech, September 2021

Haidt, Jonathon, "Why the Past Ten Years of American Life Have Been Uniquely Stupid," *The Atlantic*, April, 2022

Hopkins, Hop, "Racism Is Killing the Planet: The ideology of white supremacy leads the way toward disposable people and a disposable natural world," *Sierra Club*, June 2020

Jabr, Ferris, "How Humanity Unleashed a Flood of New Diseases," *The New York Times Magazine*, June 17, 2020

Junod, Tom, "The Falling Man," *Esquire*, September 9, 2021, https://www.esquire.com/news-politics/a48031/the-falling-man-tom-junod/

Mounk, Yascha, "The Virus Will Win: Americans are pretending that the pandemic is over. It certainly is not," *The Atlantic*, June, 2020

Staff, 9:11, "The Truth Behind the Famous Falling Man and His Real Identity," *The New Zealand Herald*, 2020, https://www.nzherald.co.nz/world/911-the-truth-behind-the-famous-falling-man-and-his-real-identity/LUON3GKFWRAEQMDVZV574IHZSY/

Yong, Ed, "Our Pandemic Summer," *The Atlantic*, April 14, 2020, https://www.theatlantic.com/health/archive/2020/04/pandemic-summer-coronavirus-reopening-back-normal/609940/

RELIGION, SPIRITUALITY AND SECULAR STUDIES

Darwin, Charles, *On the Origin of the Species*, 150th anniversary edition, Signet, 2013

Fox, Matthew, *The Coming of the Cosmic Christ*, Harper and Row Publishers, 1988

Fox, *Creation Spirituality, Liberating Gifts for the Peoples of the Earth*, Harper, 1991

King James Version, Holy Bible

McConnell, Jim, *An Introduction to Celtic Spirituality in Ireland*, 2016, unpublished manuscript

Moore, Thomas, *The Re-Enchantment of Everyday Life*, Harper Perennial, 1997

O'Donohue, John, *Anam Cara, A Book of Celtic Wisdom*, Harper Perennial, 1997

Oliver, Mary, *Upstream, Selected Essays*, Penguin Press, 2016

Rigney, Ann, *Remembering Hope: Transnational Activism beyond the Traumatic*, Memory Studies, July 7, 2018

Ritchie, Fiona, and Doug Orr, *Wayfaring Strangers: The Musical Voyage from Scotland and Ulster to Appalachia*, University of North Carolina Press, 2014

Sartre, Jean-Paul and Priest, Stephen, ed., *Jean-Paul Sartre: Basic Writings*, Routledge, 2002

Solnit, Rebecca, *A Field Guide to Getting Lost*, Penguin Books, 2016

Taylor, Bron, "Religion and Environmental Behaviour (part two): Dark-green Nature Spiritualities and the Fate of the Earth," *Ecological Citizen* 2(3), 2020: 135–140

Taylor, Bron, "Religion and Environmental Behaviour (part one): World Religions & the Fate of the Earth," *Ecological Citizen* 3(1), 2019: 71–76

Weiner, Mark, "Where Heaven and Earth Come Closer, Thin Places, Where We Are Jolted Out of Old Ways of Seeing the World, *The New York Times*, March 9, 2022

Wexler, Jay, *When God Isn't Green*, Beacon Press 2016

ABOUT THE AUTHOR

RUBY McCONNELL is a writer, geologist, and environmental activist whose award-winning work has been featured in Ms. Magazine, the Wall Street Journal, Huffington Post, Alta Journal, and Mother Earth News. She is the author of the critically-acclaimed outdoor series *A Woman's Guide to the Wild* and *A Girl's Guide to the Wild* and its companion activity book for young adventurers, and *Ground Truth: A Geological Survey of a Life*, which was a finalist for the 2020 Oregon Book Award. She lives and writes in the heart of Oregon country. You can almost always find her in the woods. @rubygonewild